The Myth of Africa

The Myth of Africa

dorothy hammond
& alta jablow

the library of social science
new york

To LORD GREYSTOKE

foreword to the new edition

This new edition of *The Myth of Africa* has been issued as a work of fundamental insight; and as a book which contributes, we feel, toward the development of a new approach in sociology which views cultural beliefs and conceptions of social reality as growing out of the *shared phantasies* of groups of persons.

Africa is, of course, a real place, which consists of real human beings. What Jablow and Hammond demonstrate in this work is that the perception of this place, and of these human beings, has its source, not only in the objective situation, but in the *unconscious phantasies which are projected into this situation.*

Using 400 years of British writing, fiction and non-fiction, as their data, the authors reconstruct the *Myth of Africa,* a coherent pattern of beliefs and imagery which has been associated with the African people and the African continent. This "myth," it would appear, defines the manner in which Africa is perceived, and, therefore, is a *fundamental determinant of the kinds of reality-encounters which are possible;* is a fundamental determinant, in short, of collective patterns of behavior *vis a vis* Africa and the black man.

The authors do not articulate, in this work, a theoretical point of view. The material which they have presented contributes, however, I believe, toward the development of a new conception of the sociology of knowledge: a conception of the sociology of knowledge which views human beliefs and perceptions of social reality as representing a *cognitive transformation of shared unconscious phantasies.*

Human beliefs and conceptions of social reality, according to this view, come into being, assume a certain form, and are perpetuated as elements of human culture, not, primarily, because they are "functional" for the society, or for a particular "class," but because they permit individuals within the society to *project unconscious phantasies into the external world.*

The Myth of Africa is the study of a particular human phantasy: the *Western phantasy of Africa.* This myth, this phantasy, as a fundamental source of the world's response to the black man, is a fundamental determinant, we may suggest, of the *history* of the black man: collective modes of behavior *vis a vis* Africa, and the Negro, reflect the *acting out of a shared unconscious phantasy.*

RICHARD A. KOENIGSBERG
January, 1977

While it may seem a departure from the usual anthropological objectives, interest in and concern with a people's views of other and alien ways of life has had a long and honorable tenure in anthropology. In a sense, any anthropological research into early writings has been of this nature, since the culturally determined biases of the writer are so much a part of how he sees and what he reports. The modern researcher must learn to distinguish relevant data from biased observations. Such research eventually led us to a concern with the nature, not so much of the data, but of the modifying biases themselves.

We began our work on the Western fantasy of Africa in 1960 with two articles published in the periodical, *Africa Today*. These articles indicated the existence of a governing literary tradition in the European and American popular writing on Africa. Each of us had also written a doctoral thesis on separate aspects of this broad problem. The articles and dissertations proved to be the seedbed for this book. While our basic idea of a Western fantasy based on ethnocentrism still prevails, much new data has been added, and with the passage of time and further study, our views of the problems have changed their shape. Our original concepts have been rethought, redefined, and greatly modified.

Our approaches and points of view have been, throughout, so totally compatible, and our collaboration of such a nature, that it is impossible for us to now distinguish any individual contribution or idea. Thus, we must both share an equal responsibility for the entire work.

There was no need to treat fiction and nonfiction separately since both are governed by the same tradition. The fiction, however, does give more forceful phrasing to the images because of the concentration of each novel upon a single complex of images. Marguerite Steen, for example, focuses on the image of Africa as dark, alien, and evil. With this imagery she elaborates upon the conventions of the brooding and implacable jungle and the uncanny powers of African witchcraft. Richard Llewellyn's *A Man in a Mirror* stresses the image of Africa as an open sunlit land inhabited by "noble savages." Nonfiction is more apt to include diverse images, none as fully developed as in the more integrated works of fiction.

Fictional and nonfictional treatments of African material differ only in respect to greater or lesser consistency and integration. The fiction is by no means more fanciful than the nonfiction. Of the following passages the second and the fourth are from novels, the first and third from nonfiction:

The stagnation of Africa is chiefly due to that jealous tribal law which forbade any man to be wiser or cleverer or richer than his neighbors. For thousands of years, Africa, like a modern dictator, has oppressed the natural freedom of the mind, and thrown away all its increase.[1]

Ibu . . . was an intelligent child. This quality had probably been her ruin. All intelligent, good-looking persons are exposed to jealousy, and jealousy is the subconscious source of the hatred which produces injurious fear; and from fear, an accusation of witchcraft. In this way Africa has destroyed every year for some millions of years, a large proportion of its more intelligent and handsome children.[2]

Africans have remained for thousands of years at virtually the same level of culture. They seem almost alone among the major races of the world to have halted in the stone age, too comfortable to go any further.[3]

People who have lived precisely the same way for hundreds of years, because they have discovered a corporate existence, which wholly satisfies them.[4]

Analysis of the images pointed up still another regularity. It became obvious that there existed a dependent correlation between the image of the Africans and that of the British. One is in reciprocal contrast to the other. Where the British are brave, the Africans are cowardly; where the Africans are carefree, the British are beset by many anxieties; where the British are gracious in granting favors, the Africans accept them without gratitude. The literature on Africa does present a very clear self-view of the British in Africa. To test the validity of this self-image we turned to commentaries and observations on British character and society. They conformed to the British self-view in the African literature. Our last chapter treats in detail the British self-view. Some readers may prefer to read this chapter first.

There are those who share none of the responsibility for the finished product, but who nevertheless contributed to its completion. We must first express our deepest gratitude to Professor Joseph Jablow for the initial impetus he provided, and for many years of patient support, advice, and encouragement. We are grateful to Professor Alexander Lesser for his sound advice and needed exhortations. We should also like to take this opportunity to express our belated thanks to our dissertation advisers, Professors Conrad Arensberg, Morton Fried, and Charles Wagley. Finally, we owe a tremendous debt of gratitude to Carl Withers for his painstaking reading of the manuscript and his many valuable suggestions.

contents

introduction

Since classical times Africa has exerted a powerful hold on the European imagination. The ancient world knew little of Africa other than Egypt and the Mediterranean littoral. Imagination transformed the rest of the continent to a strange and wonderful land where were to be found tailed men, men with heads beneath their breasts, and men who did not dream. To this classical heritage were added in time tales of other prodigies and of great riches. It was interest in the fabulous as much as interest in geography that spurred Prince Henry of Portugal to send his ships in exploration of the lands lying southward. In the sixteenth century the British followed the lead of the Portuguese and voyaged to Africa to fill their pockets and the coffers of Elizabeth's treasury. European exploration and expansion brought sober fact to dispel the old legends, but new legends took their place. Africa remained a field for the free play of European fantasy.

Western literature provides the record of the fantasy, and because it is a lurid fantasy, it has resulted in a sensational literature. It has always had wide popular appeal, especially for young readers. This literature was, in fact, the path which led us ultimately to our interest in African anthropology. Sir Henry M. Stanley along with Tarzan and Allan Quatermain were our most unlikely guides to the scientific study of African cultures. But anthropology is intolerant of fantasy, and we found ourselves looking at the literature that had given us so much pleasure with coldly professional eyes.

There are two Africas, different and incompatible: the Africa of anthropology and that of popular "literary" conception. Anthropology discerns an Africa infinitely varied, complex, and changing, inhabited by people neither more nor less human than anyone else. The anthropological view of Africa has always been subject

13

to revision as knowledge increased. In popular writing Africa is strangely homogeneous and static; differences between past and present and between one place and another are obliterated. Africans, limited to a few stock figures, are never completely human, and Africa exhibits few changes over time. It became and remains the Africa of H. Rider Haggard and Joseph Conrad. In short, the literary image of Africa is a fantasy of a continent and a people that never were and could never be.

Films also have familiarized Westerners with an Africa composed of the old notions of the Dark Continent inhabited by archetypal figures: howling savages, faithful servants, sinister half-breeds, white hunters, and gallant colonial officials. In the face of their appeal, durability, and pervasiveness, reality has little chance of acceptance.

With few exceptions, no matter how different in style, form, or content, the books—and naturally the films based upon them—present the same fantasy of Africa. With remarkable consistency the fantasy is expressed through the same idioms and figures of speech. These rhetorical devices may seem merely a manner or style of writing about Africa. Yet by persistent reiteration, a manner of speaking can become the substance of what is said. In book after book about Africa identical images appear expressing similar attitudes and concepts, often similarly phrased. Literary license allows each author to depict Africa in much the same way as every other author. Such conformity cannot be the result of chance. It clearly indicates a governing literary tradition, quite different from the tradition guiding the scientific writing.

Distinction between the two traditions is possible only for recent times. Trained anthropological observation in the field began only in the early part of the twentieth century. Before then, armchair theorists relied on the literature of voyage and exploration to supply their raw data, which was too often inadequate as well as biased. The study of man has moved steadily toward emancipation from the inevitable errors stemming from reliance on amateur and secondary sources. However, what has been discarded as unreliable by anthropology has been retained in the popular literature. The errors and biases so perpetuated have by now acquired an inviolable tenure.

Africa of the popular literature is a myth, but myths have a place and function in the societies which create them. They support cultural values and mediate points of stress. Within this context of social reality myth is subject to anthropological study. This book is an attempt to analyze the British myth of Africa, to trace its historical development, to establish its modern usages, and to indicate its relationship to other aspects of British life.

Although the British were not alone in creating a myth of Africa, we chose, for a number of reasons, to concentrate on the British writing on Africa. The British were the predominant European colonial power in Africa. In sheer volume their popular literature far exceeded that of any other nation, and much of what they wrote was accessible to us. An obvious advantage in dealing with the English material was that problems of translation were eliminated. Moreover, the investigation of the historical development of the tradition has been possible because four centuries of British contact with Africa has produced not only an enormous literature but one of unbroken continuity.

The literature of this popular tradition yields relatively little empirical knowledge about either Africa or the history of the British in Africa. Reality is nearly irrelevant to the tradition. What is relevant, and indeed, integral to it, is ethnocentrism. This means that all perception is made through the lenses of one's own system of values and beliefs. An ethnocentric point of view admits only one valid way of life. Cultures which differ from one's own are perceived as negations of that single set of values, rather than as expressions of other and different systems. Those who do not worship the God of the Christians are not necessarily worshiping the Devil of the Christians; they may be adherents of a religion to which the tenets of Christianity are totally irrelevant. Ethnocentrism, however, does not permit the possibility of alternative and perhaps equally valid ways of life. A literature dominated by ethnocentrism is bound to be unrealistic in its omissions and misinterpretations.

It is not going too far to say that ethnocentrism is a nearly universal human attitude. All people are so thoroughly conditioned to their own culture that their habits and learned modes of behavior seem the inevitable expression of basic human nature.

Other people with different habits acquired from their cultures seem to behave unnaturally or perversely. This is the basis of all preconception about alien cultures and the seedbed of the stereotypes by which they are described. Differences are almost always exaggerated. Even in the absence of difference, strange and unnatural behavior is projected onto the alien group simply because they *are* alien. These are not random projections, but reflect important and dearly held values of the perceiver. Alien behavior is made to serve as an object lesson—the contrast that highlights and affirms the worth of one's own patterns of behavior. Thus, ethnocentrism produces myths of aliens that often seem to be antagonistic, even if hostility was not intended.

Katherine George describes the European view of Africa in the literature prior to the nineteenth century as an "antagonistic fantasy."[1] She refers primarily to Dutch, Italian, and Portuguese materials, and only minimally to English accounts. Her work indicates that all the Europeans were equally biased about Africa, and their literatures reflect those biases. This remains equally characteristic of the literatures of the nineteenth and twentieth centuries.

The British view of Africa appears to be, at best, quite absurd, and at worst, the results of malice and cynicism. Yet the British have been neither malicious nor cynical; they have merely been ethnocentric. The absurdity lies in the nature of ethnocentrism itself.

With no hope of being exhaustive we have read and analyzed some five hundred volumes of fiction and nonfiction covering the period from earliest British contact with Africa in the mid-sixteenth century to the present. Our focus is on the image of Negro Africa. We have, therefore, excluded works dealing with the Sahara and North Africa since they are better understood within the context of the Moslem world. We have intentionally omitted the early works of British explorers of Ethiopia; they are sufficiently distinctive to constitute a subtradition. The modern protest literature on race relations, mainly in South Africa, has also been omitted as not directly germane to our purpose.

Writers were not and could not be selected for literary merit. There are, therefore, many more "bad" writers than "good" ones in the sample. The better writers handle the conventions with greater skill and subtlety, but all conform to the literary traditions.

The continuing dominance of the tradition can be partly accounted for by its acceptance as the only appropriate way to write about Africa. Authenticity seems assured when a writer gives his narrative "verisimilitude" by using the expected conventional images. In addition, it cannot be denied that the conventions impart a color and vitality which can rescue otherwise dull narratives. Thus, it is no wonder that so many writers continue to incorporate this useful tradition into so variegated a literature.

The British have written about Africa in many literary forms. In the earliest contact period and for a long time after, the predominant type of literature was the narrative of trade and exploration. As the British became increasingly committed to Africa there appeared many new kinds of writing: polemic tracts and romances dealing with the issues of slavery and colonialism, memoirs and reminiscences, accounts of travel on the Dark Continent, and an ever-increasing number of novels. Fiction (aside from the anti-slavery romances of the eighteenth and nineteenth centuries) did not really hit its stride until the end of the nineteenth century; by the middle of the twentieth century it was the outstanding type of popular writing about Africa.

The wide range of styles and genres presented the problem of dealing with a very heterogeneous body of material. It was, nevertheless, possible to abstract striking regularities from these works. The fundamental and unifying theme is the confrontation between Great Britain and Africa. The continent, the Africans, and the British themselves are depicted by sets of interlocking images that are consistently employed throughout the literature. These images are built up out of a stock of stereotypes formulated in highly conventional idioms and metaphors. The typical form is the narrative of travel which appeared from the beginning of British contact and has continued to the most recent present. Travel ranges from the standard trek on foot to travel in every possible conveyance: hammock, bathchair, sedan, jeep, motor bicycle, and even a balloon. It is quite rare to encounter a book in which the protagonists stay in one place. So entrenched is this convention that even books dealing with quite other matters incorporate a journey. A love story or an account of medical practice must be so written as to describe some travel. This form is appropriate to the focus of interest upon the British protagonist, whether in fact or fiction, for a journey provides a variety of African stimuli. Obviously, the more exciting and varied the stimuli, the more excited are the responses, and the livelier the book.

We have allowed direct quotations from many sources to illustrate the nature of the conventions. Generally, one or two citations must stand for an almost limitless supply, and our selection of the most suitable quotation from among such riches was often an agonizing decision. Though we might have illustrated each convention by citations from any number of writers, not every writer uses all the conventions—only those appropriate to his book. The preponderance of material from a limited group of writers should not be taken to indicate that they alone made such comments, but that we preferred their particular phrasing.

Our study of over four centuries of British writing about Africa has disclosed elements of both continuity and change. For each period certain historical factors determined the precise content of the images. These factors include the nature of British-African contact and of the personnel and the particular ideology of a given period. Yet the continuities are far more striking than the changes, since they are the result of the unifying and constant force of ethnocentrism. Ethnocentrism created and preserved until today a persistent fantasy: the civilized Briton in confrontation with savage Africans in an Africa that never was.

chapter one
first light on the dark continent

Commerce in Commodities and Human Beings: 1530–1800

BRITISH contact with Africa began in the mid-sixteenth century as part of the developing commerce between the European maritime nations and the coastal states of West Africa. From the first recorded British voyage of William Hawkins in 1530 to the early nineteenth-century voyages of exploration, British relations with Africa were dominated by the concerns of trade. Initially small in scope and sporadic in nature, the trade was in the West African commercial staples of ivory, pepper, and gold. These early ventures were profitable; John Lok's voyage of 1554 returned ten times the capital invested,[1] and William Towerson exchanged a "copper Bason" for gold equivalent to thirty pounds sterling.[2]

The earliest literature clearly reflects the overwhelming preoccupation with trade. It is a sparse literature and consists of brief accounts of trading voyages in Richard Hakluyt and Samuel Purchas,[3] and a few separate accounts such as the one by Richard Jobson.[4] The narratives emphasize the details and mechanics of trade: compass and sailing directions, lists of place names, and items bought and sold. The new land and its people were only incidentally described, and then within the limited geographical range of a few coastal areas. British writing of this early period nowhere indicates an interest in the life of the Africans equal to that of the Dutch and Portuguese writers of the same period.

British accounts briefly described the location, topography, and climate of the coastal areas, casually noted the novel flora and fauna, and briefly commented on the people. Occasionally the writers larded their own sketchy observations with borrowings from classical writers. For example, Eden's account of the voyage captained by Lok in 1561 mingles observed details with fantasy from the classical tradition.

> . . . Negroes, a people of beastly living, without a God, lawe, religion, or common wealth. . . . There also other people . . . whose women are common: for they contract no matrimonie, neither have respect to chastitie . . . the region called Troglodytica, whose inhabitants dwel in caves and dennes: for these are their houses, and the flesh of serpents their meat, as writeth Plinie, and Diodorus Siculus. They have no speach, but rather a grinning and chattering. There are also people without heads . . . having their eyes and mouths in their breast. . . . Among other things therefore, touching the maners and nature of the people, this may seeme strange, that their princes and noble men use to punce and rase their skinnes with pretie knots in divers formes. . . . And albeit they goe in maner all naked, there are many of them, and especially their women, in maner laden with collars, bracelets, hoopes, and chaines either of gold, copper or ivory. I my selfe have one of their braslets of Ivory. . . .[5]

In general, the early British traders seem to have found the Africans strange and perhaps not entirely to their liking, but they were viewed as real or potential partners in a commercial arrangement in which the British recognized their own dependence upon them. The writers did not engage in polemics or invidious comparisons; even when they indicated distaste at what they saw, it was not made an occasion for moral judgment. Certainly the Africans were savages, but one could trade as profitably with savages as with anyone else; and these particular savages were just as eager as the British to engage in commerce. As trade partners they were respected; for, savage or not, they were shrewd traders and skillful bargainers. Eden, in recounting Lok's voyage, found them to be

> . . . very wary people in their bargaining, [who] will not lose one sparke of golde of any value. They use weights and measures, and are very circumspect in occupying the same. They that shall have to doe with them must use them gently; for they will not trafique or bring in any wares, if they be evill used.[6]

Towerson's comment indicates how tightly organized the African traders were in this period.

> The 16. day in the morning we went into the river with our Skiffe, and tooke some of every sort of our merchandize with us, and shewed it to the Negroes, but they esteemed it not . . . so that this day we tooke not by estimation above one hundredth poundweight of Graines, by meanes of their Captaine, who would suffer no man to sell anything but through his hands, and at his price: he was so subtile, that for a bason he would not give 15. pound weight of Graines . . . and when he saw that wee would not take them in contentment, the Captaine departed and caused all the rest of the boates to depart. . . .[7]

Aside from a few displays of reading in the classics, this is a matter-of-fact literature, and in a matter-of-fact way it adumbrates the image of the continent as the White Man's Grave. The most portentous statistics deal not with profits but with disease and death. In this early period, the history of the British on the West Coast often reads like a series of death notices: "And of seven score men came home to Plimmouth scarcely forty. . . ."[8] Towerson, writing of his third voyage, states that "The crews began to fall sick even before the Mina coast was reached"; on the way home by way of the Cape Verde Islands, the crews of three ships were reduced to only "30 sound men."[9]

The gains from commodities paled into insignificance beside the enormous profits made from the buying and selling of slaves. The British slave trade began on a very small scale in the 1560's with several voyages of John Hawkins to the "coast of Guinea . . . where he got into his possession, partly by the sword and partly by other meanes, to the number of three hundred Negroes. . . ."[10] From then on the continuity and growth of the slave trade were ensured; its enormous rewards far outweighed the high risks. By the beginning of the eighteenth century British trade with Africa had become almost exclusively a trade in slaves.

The British merchants bought their slaves from African traders, who in turn obtained them in the interior, a time-honored practice which established the middle-man position of the African coastal chiefs. This procedure effectively limited the British to the littoral and restricted their contacts mainly to their African suppliers.

The chiefs were anxious to prevent Europeans from penetrating the hinterland, afraid that they might gain influence and eventual control of the mainland trade. Up to the nineteenth century, in fact, the African chiefs and traders had the upper hand; their power was sufficiently strong to check the growth of British power and to limit the British area of operations.

The dangers of travel in the interior also prevented inland expansion. The dense rain forest and the untraversable swamps were formidable obstacles, and the ever-present fever was, perhaps, an even greater deterrent. Besides, the British merchants were interested above all in their profits. As long as these were forthcoming, there was no compelling motive to brave the hazards of the interior. Small wonder, then, that as late as the beginning of the nineteenth century, the sum of British holdings in West Africa consisted of the tiny colonies at Freetown and Gambia, maintained precariously by traders with government aid, and a string of forts and factories along the coast, held largely on leasehold and at the sufferance of local chiefs.

By mid-eighteenth century certain aspects of the British situation in West Africa had changed. The hitherto powerful competition of the Dutch and Portuguese had finally been eliminated by the Treaty of Utrecht. The trade was no longer hit-and-run, for the British were ensconced in relatively permanent trading posts along the coast from the Senegal River to the Oil Rivers. They could support an established and settled trade, although their operations were still clearly dependent upon the good will of the Africans.

Accounts of British activity in Africa during the eighteenth century are contained in J. Churchill's compendium[11] and in several individual works: Robert Norris and Archibald Dalzel both recorded their observations of the Kingdom of Dahomey, and William Smith and William Snelgrave recounted their voyages to Guinea.[12] Continuity with the earlier writing was maintained; the emphasis was still on trade and its circumstances. But there was a marked change in the tenor of the literature. Its content shifted from almost indifferent and matter-of-fact reports of what the voyagers had seen to judgmental evaluation of the Africans. John Phillips, a trader of this period, referred to the "swinish manner" of the Negroes and their "murderous treachery." [13] Dalzel described the king of Dahomey as a cruel and bloody tyrant,[14] and Norris concurred.

. . . and he sports with [his subjects], with the most savage and wanton cruelty. Piles of their heads are placed as ornaments before his palace . . . and the floors leading to his apartments are strewed with their bodies. . . .[15]

Eighteenth-century comments placed inordinate emphasis upon the sanguinary aspects of West African cultures. African behavior, institutions, and character were not merely disparaged but presented as the negation of all human decencies. African religions were vile superstition; governments but cruel despotism; polygyny was not marriage, but the expression of innate lusts. The shift to such pejorative comment was due in large measure to the effects of the slave trade. A vested interest in the slave trade produced a literature of devaluation, and since the slave trade was under attack, the most derogatory writing about Africans came from its literary defenders. Dalzel, for instance, prefaced his work with an apologia for slavery: "Whatever evils the slave trade may be attended with . . . it is mercy . . . to poor wretches, who . . . would otherwise suffer from the butcher's knife." [16] Numerous proslavery tracts appeared, all intent upon showing the immorality and degradation of Africans. Basil Davidson cites an anonymous pamphlet from eighteenth-century Liverpool to this effect.

Africans being the most lascivious of all human beings, may it not be imagined that the cries they let forth at being torn from their wives, proceed from the dread that they will never have the opportunity of indulging their passions in the country to which they are embarking? [17]

Enslavement of such a degraded people was thus not only justifiable but even desirable. The character of Africans could change only for the better through contact with their European masters. Slavery, in effect, became the means of the Africans' salvation, for it introduced them to Christianity and civilization.

The slave trade was the subject of bitter controversy. People of diverse beliefs and backgrounds united in opposition to slavery, and their protest eventually achieved its abolition in the early nineteenth century. The leading spokesmen for the antislavery movement included such forceful personalities as William Wilberforce, James Fox, John Wesley, Harriet Martineau, Hannah More, and Sir Charles and Lady Middleton. Theirs was a direct approach, concerned with the philosophical and moral issues in slavery. They wrote tracts, made speeches, and engaged in political action. In short, they produced a literature of abolition, but it did not contribute to the image of Africa.

There were, however, among the publicists of the antislavery movement—along with less well-known writers—a group of the most distinguished literary figures of England, such men as Daniel Defoe, Joseph Addison, Thomas Day, Thomas Chatterton, William Cowper, and Samuel Johnson. As the antislavery campaign entered the nineteenth century, its adherents included almost every distinguished novelist and poet of the times. These professional literati embellished their antislavery writing with literary inventions and created a new Africa inhabited by a new breed of Africans.

For the White Man's Grave inhabited by beastly savages, the antislavery writers substituted an Arcadian landscape where dwelt people of the greatest nobility, beauty, and refinement. In the light of modern knowledge the available accounts of Africa may not seem the height of factual realism, but in the eighteenth century such accounts provided all the "facts" there were. It was a remarkable literary feat to have put aside all data and to have completely transcended the "facts." The following description by Michel Adanson, an eighteenth-century voyager, is a model of the antislavery idylls of African life:

Which way soever I turned my eyes, I behold a perfect image of pure nature: an agreeable solitude bounded on every side by a charming landscape; the rural situation of cottages in the midst of trees; the ease and quietness of the negroes . . . temperate, moral religiously inclined folk, intelligent and industrious. . . .[18]

Robert Burns, safe in Scotland, succumbed to the geographical vagaries about Africa in his compassionate "Slave's Lament."

It was in sweet Senegal that my foes did me enthrall
For the lands of Virginia, O;
Torn from that lovely shore, and must never see it more,
And also I am weary, weary, O!

All on that charming coast is not bitter snow or frost,
Like the lands of Virginia, O;
There streams forever flow, and there flowers forever blow,
And also I am weary, weary, O! [19]

The motives of these writers were clear enough. One of the pro-slavery arguments was that the coast was so pestilential that it could only benefit the Africans to remove them to more whole-some lands. This argument was countered by a bold denial from the antislavery writers. Their Africa was thoroughly salubrious; it thus could not constitute a kindness to take people away from rural delights. In the employ of polemics, the literary imagination created a pseudo-Africa.

The antislavery writers created a pseudo-African to dwell in pseudo-Africa. Counter to the "beastly savage" of the slavers was the "noble savage" of the antislavery romancers. The noble savage is a well-established literary figure, a device often used in criticism of the writer's society. The convention proposes that man in na-ture is free, innocent, and virtuous. Uncorrupted by civilization he is naturally noble in character. This very old literary contrast be-tween natural virtue and civilized vice received new formulation as a by-product of the Age of Discovery. The explorers Sir Francis Drake, Sir Walter Raleigh, and Philip Amadas seemingly with an eye toward promoting colonization, praised the virtues of savage men in savage lands. Elizabethan drama and poetry began to laud exotic heroes. William Shakespeare's Othello and Christopher Marlowe's Tamburlaine were more than life-sized exemplars of the devotion and valor of barbaric noblemen.

The noble-savage convention came late to Africa with Mrs. Aphra Behn's novelette, *Oroonoko*. Othello may have been the model for Oroonoko, but Oroonoko himself was the undisputed antecedent for innumerable African romances of the noble-savage genre. The hero, an African prince of royal blood and bearing, and his equally royal love, Imoinda, are captured and enslaved.

Their tribulations at the hands of brutal white men and their heroic deaths constitute the plot of the tale. It was dramatized by Thomas Southerne in 1696 and appeared in many other adaptations through the eighteenth century. From 1696 to 1801 some version of the play was performed in England every year. Apart from actual adaptations of the Oroonoko tale there were even more imitations of it, all immensely popular and confirming the presence of noble savages in Africa.

Oroonoko and his like were taken up with enthusiasm by the abolitionists as suitable vehicles for antislavery propaganda. Antislavery sentiment provided a new function for the noble-savage romance. Its role shifted from a critique of civilization to an attack upon slavery. What justice or humanity could there be in the cruel enslavement of such a noble figure as Oroonoko?

The most illustrious courts could not have produced a braver man, both for Greatness of Courage and Mind, a Judgement more solid, a Wit more quick, and a Conversation more sweet and diverting. . . . He had an extreme good and graceful Mien, and all the Civility of a well-bred Great Man.[20]

European attitudes toward nobility were pivotal in selecting those virtues granted the noble savage. He was depicted as the counterpart of the contemporary English aristocrat. The "noble savage" and the "beastly savage" were conventions equally lacking in realism; both represented opposite poles on the single scale of English values. As the noble savage epitomized the ideal of British character, so the beastly savage was its antithesis. The symbolism also pertained to physical appearance. The beastly savage was disgustingly ugly. The noble savage was, on the other hand, the beau ideal of manly beauty, wanting only a light skin to be entirely perfect. We again return to that paragon, Oroonoko, for illustration.

He was . . . of a Shape the most exact that can be fancy-d: The most famous Statuary could not form the Figure of a Man more admirably turn-d from head to foot. His face was not that brown rusty Black which most of that Nation are, but a perfect Ebony, polished Jett. . . . His nose was rising and Roman, instead of African and flat.

His Mouth the finest shaped that could be seen; far from those great turn-d lips which are so natural to the rest of the Negroes.[21]

The convention of the noble savage was never extended to the entire African population. All the African noble-savage heroes and heroines are princes and princesses whose nobility of character matched the aristocracy of their lineage. The fundamental impropriety and shame of slavery was the degradation of an aristocrat to servile status. Not only had the function of the noble-savage convention undergone a sea change, its basic meaning had altered. The noble savage no longer referred to natural man; "noble" described his social status quite as much as it did his character.

In the more operatic protests against slavery the common Africans barely exist. At best, the commonality is pitiable in its enslavement and suffering. Quite often, however, the lower classes appear venal and ignoble. The Reverend William Dodd wrote many poems in the noble-Negro tradition which were reprinted in numerous anthologies. His regal Africans disdain the "rabble of ordinary slaves of manners brutish who mock'd my sufferings and my pangs renew'd, and lament the humiliations of enslaved *royalty*" (italics ours).[22] Thus, at least in part, the noble-Negro romance incorporates the more pervasive major convention of the beastly savage.

Aside from the fantasy of the classical tradition, there were no set conventions from which the early British writers on Africa could draw. They did utilize the pattern of ethnocentric description which characterized the literature on other "savage" peoples, such as the American Indian.[23] The usual ethnocentrism in writing about non-Europeans and the special context of the slave trade gave rise to the dual conventions which form the basic themes of the tradition to be echoed and elaborated through the years.

The Early Nineteenth Century: West Africa

The extremely lucrative traffic in slaves was legally terminated early in the nineteenth century. The slave trade went on *sub rosa* for a number of years, but it had a limited future. Thus, the English traders looked for alternative commodities on the West Coast and for this reason even penetrated the forbidding hinterland.

The quest for new commodities was a compelling purpose and converged with another major current of contemporary interest: scientific geography and exploration. For the first time not all voyages to Africa were undertaken as purely mercantile ventures. The newly formed African Association's chief concern was to map the West African hinterland and to determine the exact course of the Niger River.[1] Profit and science could be served simultaneously. As new areas were explored and new people were contacted, their trade potential could be assayed and tapped.

Geographical exploration was stimulated by the Enlightenment and its scientific and humanitarian concerns. Commercial motives took on fresh value as profit-seeking was also phrased in humanitarian terms. The slave trade could be brought to an end only by the substitution of profitable trade in other commodities. It was clear that the issue of slavery and the slave trade had not disappeared with the abolition of slavery. It was, and continued to be for a long time, the major ideological theme in the literature on Africa, as part of the general motive of philanthropy. The combined motives of philanthropy, advancement of science, and development of commerce are explicitly stated by the explorer Hugh Clapperton in the beginning of his *Journal of a Second Expedition into the Interior of Africa.*

Such exploration should provide a favourable opportunity of establishing an intercourse with the interior of Africa, and probably of putting an effectual check . . . to a large portion of the infamous traffic carried on in the Bight of Benin, and also for extending the legitimate commerce of Great Britain with this part of Africa and at the same time adding to our knowledge of the country. . . .[2]

These newer motives, though more altruistic, contained the germs of condescension. The British were beginning to regard themselves as the bearers of enlightenment to the Dark Continent. This attitude was not yet fully developed, however, and is in this period almost tentatively expressed in the literature. Captain Allen of the 1841 Niger Expedition addressed the Africans with whom he was to make a trade agreement as follows:

where they might enjoy true British hospitality and comfort, if not always the elegance described here by Declé.

What struck me most was the simple elegance and good taste reigning in this pleasant household. Pretty services of china appeared at meals; spotless, well-washed, and embroidered table-linen, all so clean and well kept that you could hardly believe yourself in the heart of Africa.[34]

It is also very clear that the insistence on maintaining British standards in these homes was a response to Africa itself. The very Englishness of the home made it a needed refuge and escape from the alien qualities of the Dark Continent. Mrs. Larymore is explicit in this regard, and as the first, and for a long time, the only, Englishwoman in Northern Nigeria, she expressed her determination to resist Africa by creating a small island of home.

. . . no English housewife in West Africa—if she is "worth her salt" —will spare herself in the endeavour to, at least, turn "quarters" into "home," even if only for a few months . . . no one, I think, could resist a pathetic appeal for a pretty sketch to carry away into far Africa! And, indeed, it is a joy sometimes, when the temperature is unpleasantly high, little worries abounding, and *Africa* asserting itself unduly, to be able to glance occasionally at a sketch of some English woodland, or a corner of a picturesque village.[35]

Wherever the British were in Africa, they were now in British territory. Order was maintained by British law; personal safety was secure. Servants were trained to run British households and to speak English. The continent and its savage population was being run in British fashion. The "darkness" of Africa was being dispelled by the civilizing light of a British administration and British values.

The White Man's Burden

The new challenges and tasks of colonialism in Africa wrought changes not only in the British self-image but in their image of the continent. The former image of Africa made it the setting for a drama of personal heroism, yet it conferred upon Africa some status as an entity, however hostile and dangerous. In the new view, the continent was merely raw material to be molded skillfully into a colony that would provide a market, resources, and room for settlement. This was its challenge and its *raison d'être*. The image of Africa had been transformed from a land to be conquered into a territory to be exploited.

The writers continued to describe the physical surroundings as they had earlier; such detailing had by now become an integral part of the tradition. But there was an additional emphasis on potential. Terrain was not purely for mapping or marching over, but was to be studied with an eye for utilization and for settlement. Landscape descriptions in the flowery language of Victorian prose abruptly shift to business-like appraisal of potential worth. In the following passage on Uganda, it almost seems as if Sir Harry Johnston the artist began, only to be replaced by Sir Harry the practical administrator.

After the hot sunshine, which has played on the traveller's back as he toiled up the hill, with its red soil and very green grass, the plunge into the cool depths of forest, with their innumerable palms, wild bananas, and soaring trees with white trunks, gives a delightful sense of relief, and he is sorry when the pretty causeway of white sand comes to an end, and he must toil once more up the opposite bank of red clay. I am afraid the country being of this nature it will prove extremely expensive to construct a railway across it, though a short railway from the coast of Uganda to Ruwenzori and the south end of Lake Albert would be of immense value. . . .[1]

The literary justifications of empire in Africa were primarily directed at the British taxpayer to convince him of the worth of the new dominion. Thus the new possession was portrayed as a salubrious, picturesque, and valuable adjunct to the British Empire. The English had been writing this way about South Africa since the beginning of the nineteenth century, and it might simply have been, at the height of empire, a continuation of this earlier literary convention. It seems, however, to be more clearly an advertisement for empire, and is almost startling to find in certain descriptions of West Africa. For example, Thomas J. Alldridge, the Gov-

ernor of Sierra Leone, suddenly and incongruously transforms the
White Man's Grave into a new Zion where the Englishman might
take his ease.

Lounging in my most comfortable rokhee chair, chatting with pleasant
companions, while taking the beauty of the scenery, it was really
quite delightful; so that . . . we felt contented and at peace with
all mankind and affectionately inclined towards the West Coast of
Africa, which . . . is able to provide us with enchantingly beautiful
scenery, pure air, and most needful repose.[2]

It is impossible to ignore the factor of vested interest in the use
of this particular image. Most of the writers who stressed the ad-
vantages of Britain's new colonial acquisition had serious personal
commitments to Africa. Emphasis on the difficulties could only
contravene their own strenuous efforts to build an empire. There
is not the slightest suggestion of dishonesty in their outlook; it is
more a matter of self-delusion.

The image of Africa as a new Zion had a short life, lasting only
so long as the initial excitement about the new African colonies;
even during that period many writers continued to use the older
and more enduring image of the Dark Continent. For them, as for
the writers of the twentieth century, it was a land of mystery and
danger, a crucible for testing character. Though such depictions
were neither frequent nor elaborate, they cropped up often
enough during this period to indicate the persistence of the earlier
image and to adumbrate its use in the twentieth century.

Africa always claims its forfeits; and so the four white men who had
started together from Mombasa returned but three to Cairo.[3]

. . . the West Coast of Africa . . . is a Belle Dame Sans Merci.[4]

. . . the vacant look upon our maps, which tells how long this mysterious land has kept its secrets.[5]

. . . Africa proves a man, and he who issues unscathed from that
furnace is pure gold indeed.[6]

Presently one of the liveliest conventions is that of Africa as a
preserve, and it took shape in the literature of the height of em-

pire. Partly rooted in the already familiar convention of the sportsman's paradise, it also reflected the new possessive attitudes toward the land. Conservation was the new theme: to preserve for the civilized world those features of Africa which were unique. Some writers, though rather atypically, deplored the excessive slaughter of game for fear it disappear and lessen both the beauty and the value of the colony. Aside from the promotion of settlement and tourism, the preservation of natural wonders was considered essential if Africa was to retain its most appealing qualities. What would Africa be without its herds of wild game, its dense forests, or its savage population? [7]

These were also the very features that many of the writers evoked as vestiges of primordial times. They saw Africa as a reservoir of antiquity. Churchill referred to Africa's "primeval chaos," "primary religion," and "primordial nakedness";[8] Bryce, discussing social evolution, suggested that Africa was preservative of ancient forms.[9] It is left, however, to Sir Harry Johnston to state the theme most explicitly.

The European, in fact, feels, consciously or unconsciously that he is out of his element and his age, that, as in Mr. Wells's suggestive story "The Time Machine," the wheels of time have been reversed for him, and he has been transported back to a past epoch in the earth's history, before this planet was fitted in its atmosphere and surroundings for the presence of modern man.[10]

This theme is congruent with the basic image of the Dark Continent in its emphasis on inordinately great age and primitivity. It also related to the widely accepted evolutionism which placed African cultures at the very bottom of the ladder of Progress and Civilization. Yet now that Africa was part of the British Empire it was unthinkable to the empire-builders that it be left there. The vigorous exponents of Victorian values fully intended to lift Africa from its "primeval chaos" to civilized order.

Britain's new imperial status in Africa also brought about significant changes in the image of the African people. As the land was a resource to be developed, the people were subjects to be governed and labor to be utilized—"the white man is the brain and the black man the muscle." [11] The final outcome—one that was confidently anticipated—was a profitable colony inhabited by a contented and hard-working people, moving ever toward Progress and Civilization. Whatever reservations there were about this outcome concerned the extent to which the Africans were improvable, and even these doubts were overridden with the optimism typical of the times. If the Africans were not inherently capable of attaining a higher civilization themselves, they could, as adequate and docile workers, do their bit for the general advancement of mankind.

The fulfillment of this imperial vision involved first, pacification of the territories, by treaty preferably, by arms if necessary. It was thought that military action would not be called for save against Arabs and the few intransigently militant tribes. And in these cases the British would be delivering oppressed peoples who would clearly prefer the just and humane rule of the British. Such people would reward British efforts on their behalf with open arms. In his accounts of British campaigns in Nigeria, Seymour Vandeleur described the heartwarming welcome accorded Goldie after he had defeated the Fulani overlords of the area.

. . . Sir George Goldie . . . received quite an ovation. He was met by about 2000 people, and the chief and leading people threw themselves on their knees before him, and thanked him for having rid them of their oppressors. The women and children emitted shrill shrieks of joy as each white man passed, and seemed very glad to see us. . . .[12]

In the same vein is Lugard's description of the poignant anxiety of the Toru of Uganda at the possibility of British withdrawal.

The people of Toru . . . were most eager to come under our protection. . . . Others asked me if we had come to stay; for if we should desert them as the Egyptian garrisons had deserted the people of Northern Unyoro . . . only massacre and slavery would await them. . . . I replied—how could I do otherwise?—that these countries were ceded to the British by the nations of Europe, and that the British flag never went back.[13]

Portrayal of Africans as innately servile people who had to be rescued and protected was an older convention stemming from the historical conditions of the slave trade. In the imperial tradition, however, the primary issue was not one of slavery, but of political and social subjugation. Since the African's "natural servility" made him a willing and perennial subject, it was up to the British to protect and liberate him from all exploitive despots. There was no doubt that the Africans had to be governed; they could not be left to govern themselves, and indeed, they would not want to. In this, as in other things, they were, points out Lugard, totally unlike the English (Teutons).

In Africa, moreover, there is among the people a natural inclination to submit to higher authority. That intense detestation of control which animates our Teutonic races does not exist among the tribes of Africa.[14]

The new subject status of the Africans called for a reworking of some of the older stereotypes; the Africans were now to be evaluated in terms of subordination and incorporation into a colonial system. The British were thus concerned with African docility, cooperativeness, industriousness, bellicosity, or any other characteristics pertinent to colonial efficiency.

Much more attention was paid to tribal characteristics. The generalizations about "the African" and "the Negro" were still used, usually by those with limited experience in Africa. For example, Mrs. Hall, a temporary visitor to Africa, wrote as if there were no distinction at all between one African and another; all Africans were the same, and all were innately "childlike." [15] Others who may have been far more aware of tribal differences saw them as qualities or characteristics of everyone in the tribe.

Though at first there were some differences of opinion among the writers as to what particular tribal qualities were,[16] the descriptions soon became set. In Arthur S. White's summary of African geography, resources, and people, the Africans were described only in terms of these stereotypes. White presented each tribe through a sketch of tribal character, directed toward an evaluation of the tribal role in the development of empire—their special abilities or defects, the problems they might present in the creation or maintenance of a colony. Most patently the governing of the "unstable Bechuana" and the "vigorous and independent Kaffir" would require entirely different methods, and neither would do at all for the "Jews of Africa, the enterprising and shrewd Fula." [17]

The Baganda were described by Lugard as "extremely clever in artisan work . . . and the more civilized methods of agriculture." [18] Both Johnston and Churchill called them the "Japanese of Africa" for their politeness and elegance of demeanor; and Churchill went on to say that they were "docile and intelligent, an island of gentle manners and peaceful civilization." [19] Such a depiction of the Baganda could only have been written at the end of the century. Before that they were consistently described as one of the bloodier kingdoms of Central Africa, torn by constant civil strife, ruled by a savage and bloodthirsty despot.

Since an African army was required to serve the needs of empire, tribes were appraised in regard to their military fitness. Vandeleur, himself a professional soldier, volunteered the Hausa as "sturdy-looking men and excellent marchers . . . the best fighting material in Africa." [20] Robinson knew the Hausa well, and he fully concurred in this opinion, suggesting further that the Hausa were such "splendid soldiers" because they were superior in character and temperament to the "degraded savages" of Dahomey, Ashanti, and Benin.[21] While in partial agreement with these opinions, Lugard nevertheless plumped for the Sudanese as the best soldiers; "they are brave, extremely amenable to discipline . . . having the instincts of a soldier in routine duties." [22]

African rulers, no longer possessing the power to hinder empire, were evaluated solely in terms of their potential usefulness to colonial administration. The policy of indirect rule required cooperation from native rulers, so this was the quality upon which they were judged. If the chief proved amenable and efficient in carrying out British programs he was a good chief; otherwise, he was bad.

The attitude toward the chief did not differ from that toward all Africans. The chief required some special treatment, perhaps, but only because of the usefulness of his office, not because of the deference customarily due a ruler. The descriptions of African rulers often evince contempt, sometimes politely veiled, and at other times explicit. Mary Kingsley here leavens her contempt for a West African chief by her customary jocularity.

. . . strange and highly interesting function of going to a tea-party at a police station to meet a king—a real reigning king—who kindly attended with his suite . . . Tachie (that's His Majesty's name) is an old, spare, man with a subdued manner. His sovreign rights are acknowledged by the Government so far as to hold him more or less responsible for any iniquity committed by his people; and as the Government do not allow him to execute or flagellate the said people, earthly pomp is rather a hollow thing to Tachie.[23]

If permitted to rule without government supervision the chiefs would merely perpetuate savage customs—trial by ordeal, cannibalism, human sacrifice, infanticide, and certain forms of marriage and property rights—all designated as targets for reform. Yet these very customs are given so much attention in the literature that it is clear the British were at least as fascinated as they were horrified by them.

A new fillip was added to the beastly savage conventions by many sensational tales of cannibalism. There had been, earlier, minimal interest in the subject, though it had been occasionally reported. William Snelgrave, Robert Norris, and Archibald Dalzel in the eighteenth century had referred to the cannibalistic practices in Dahomey. It was reported from West Africa in the early nineteenth century, but there is little reference to cannibalism in the literature on South Africa in that period. Exploitation of the theme began in the mid-nineteenth century. Stanley was carried away in his zealous horror of anthropophagy and repeated every tale of cannibal tribes that he heard in addition to creating quite a number of his own. Winwood Reade sprinkled cannibals about West Africa rather like raisins in a cake. Other mid-century explorers mention certain tribes as cannibalistic, relying on older reports or hearsay.

In the imperial period writers were far more addicted to tales of cannibalism than the Africans ever were to cannibalism. Its prevalence was taken for granted, and no actual evidence was required to establish that a tribe was notoriously anthropophagous. Lady

Flora Lugard postulated the existence of a "belt of cannibalism
. . . across the whole breadth of Africa." [24] Grogan, almost always more sensational than judicious, wrote his eyewitness account, only a small part of which is quoted here, of the aftermath
of a purported cannibal orgy in Mushari, a district inhabited by
the Bateka tribe.

Mushari, lined with grain and torn skins, relics of those unfortunates
who had been caught; and dried pools of blood, gaunt skeletons,
grinning skulls and trampled grass, told a truly African tale . . .
about 3000 square miles in extent had been depopulated and devas-
tated. I do not believe that 2% of the thousands of inhabitants have
survived. [25]

Modern anthropology casts considerable doubt on the extent of
cannibalism in Africa. The evidence would seem to indicate that
the practice of cannibalism was extremely circumscribed, and occurred only within the context of sorcery and witchcraft. [26] But the
writers of empire were clearly predisposed to find cannibalism
even where there was no evidence.

Besides the political value of the theme as a justification for
colonialism, the commercial value of literary sensationalism cannot be ignored as a motive for its perpetuation. Cannibal stories
were titillating enough to insure increased sales of books, and few
writers were averse to exploiting the theme. European readers are
accustomed to cannibalism as a literary theme. It is an integral
part of the fairy tales and nursery rhymes, and adults still respond
with avid interest to tales of cannibalism especially when presented as one of the "realities" of African life. So valuable an adjunct to the literary tradition was the theme of cannibalism that it
remained one of the most persistent conventions.

The most important contribution of the cannibalism theme to
the entire literary tradition is that it provides a vivid new variation of the beastly savage image of the African. It underlines in a
most dramatic fashion that African behavior is a negation of European values.

All descriptions of Africans throughout this period emphasized
traits thought to be indicative of inferiority. Ascriptions that had
been made at an earlier time to the Africans of thicker skulls,

harder heads, and insensitivity to pain were all continued in the imperial tradition. Hitherto there had been only an occasional mention of any distinctive African odor. The literature of empire, however, frequently refers to the "bouquet d'Afrique." Johnston thought it of sufficient interest to discourse "scientifically" on the nature of the "peculiar foetor." [27] A new group of stereotypes concerning the excessive fecundity and sexuality of the African appeared at this time. James Bryce and Johnston remark on these.

They are more prolific than the whites, and their increase is not restrained by those prudential checks which tell upon civilized man.[28]

. . . the concentration of their thoughts on sexual intercourse . . . is the negro's greatest weakness. Nature has probably endowed him with more than the usual generic faculty. After all, to these people almost without arts and sciences and the refined pleasures of the senses, the only acute enjoyment offered them by nature is sexual intercourse.[29]

The writers also ascribed a host of mental and moral failings to the Africans. They were ignorant as well as incapable of any intellectual attainment. They lacked any sense of time; they could not reason or think in abstract terms; and since they were without the gifts of invention or creativity, they were innately imitative. As for emotions, Africans were described as lacking all the finer feelings such as gratitude, pity, or true love, and in general they were emotionally unstable. Morally, too, they were very short of the mark since they were lazy, liars, thieves, cowards, and bullies.[30]

Underlying these attributions was the still unequivocally accepted racial determinism of mid-century, and now it was strongly supported by the doctrine of evolution. Popularized versions of Darwinism were apparently so congruent with the temper of the times as to require no amplification, defense, or argument. Evolution provided a tailor-made and facile explanation of the Africans' place in nature and in society.

The typical late nineteenth-century statement concerning the evolutionary position of the African placed him on the lowest rungs of the evolutionary ladder. Bryce's evolutionary scheme posited secure pigeonholes for all varieties of mankind—tribe by tribe—and if some African tribes were more advanced than others, all ranked well down on the scale.

As their religious customs were rather less sanguinary than those of the Guinea Coast negroes, so the Kaffirs themselves were somewhat more advanced in civilization. Compared with the Red Indians of America, they stood at a point lower than that of the Iroquois or Cherokees, but superior to the Utes or to the Diggers of the Pacific Coast.[31]

Bryce's scheme contains more literary than scientific merit, but it, at least, has the virtue of retaining the Africans within the confines of humanity. Others believed that the Africans had not yet, or only just, come down out of the trees, and were far more akin to monkeys and apes than to man. Grogan even discovered an entirely new and improbable tribe of

. . . ape-like creatures . . . quite distinct from the other peoples. . . . Their face, body and limbs are covered with wiry hair and the hang of the long powerful arms, the slight stoop of the trunk, and the hunted, vacant expression of the face made up a *tout ensemble* that was terrible pictorial proof of Darwinism.[32]

Nineteenth-century theories of Social Darwinism, racism, and biological determinism provided justification for the initial conquest and subsequent domination of Africa. According to the tenet of "survival of the fittest," which was, for the layman, the most outstanding aspect of evolution, conquest was self-validating. The innate inferiority of the conquered was demonstrated by the fact that they *were* conquered and could be accounted for by their unfitness in the evolutionary contest. The inevitable concomitant of these assumptions was developed in colonial policy—the European had to assume responsibility for the governing and welfare of the inferior peoples.

The evolutionary schemes propounded by the writers of empire were grounded in racism. Differences in culture, history, language, and behavior were confounded with biological differences, and even when they were able to distinguish among them, the writers attributed all differences to the crucial factor of race; thus evolutionary development, too, was seen as a function of racial difference. Restatements of the biblical concept of the Negroes' descent from Ham do not appear in the literature of empire as frequently as they had earlier, but theories of polygenesis flourished, most of them indicating that the Negro belonged to an entirely different and lesser species. This is the substance of Mary Kingsley's comment that ". . . the difference between the African and [the European] is a difference not of degree but of kind. . . . I feel certain that a black man is no more an undeveloped white man than a rabbit is an undeveloped hare." [33]

The rationalization of empire and white supremacy was predicated upon the assumption of vast differences between the British and their African subjects. The philanthropic-minded among the British may have been concerned that the gulf between them was so great, but nowhere was it altogether denied, and for the most part it was considered inevitable, permanent, and even essential. Bryce was one of many who believed that even the Africans accepted it as the natural order.

. . . the black man accepts the superiority of the white as part of the order of nature. He is too low down, too completely severed from the white, to feel indignant. Even the few educated natives are too well aware of the gulf that divides their own people from the European to resent . . . the attitude of the latter.[34]

Westernized Africans represented some lessening of the disparity between the two cultures and hence were seen as a source of disruption of the natural order. They were viewed with suspicion and hostility; the British seem angered at what amounted to African presumption at having attempted to bridge the gulf. Emotion and theory parted company at this point; the Africans were to be guided toward progress, but at the pace and under conditions dictated by the British. It was too soon for any visible signs of progress, and the Westernized African represented too quick a leap. A frequent concomitant of the attitude of hostility toward the Westernized African was a nostalgic expression of preference for the simple savage, untouched by progress. Thus Lionel Declé comments.

Black gentlemen . . . were to be met with in the grog shops, the headquarters of the Salvation Army and the gaols . . . they served only to show the result of the devolution of a fine savage into a degraded, European-dressing, hard-drinking, work-hating . . . black-looking villain: for such is the free-born, dark-skinned citizen loafer of the Cape Colony, the proud and respected owner of a vote.[35]

It is paradoxical that the agents of progress and civilization should have expressed such a preference for the "fine savage" untouched by their influence. The paradox can be resolved by recognition of the nature of British attitudes toward subject peoples in general and toward the Negro in particular. The Westernized African contravened the clear-cut distinctions the British had drawn and intended to maintain between themselves and the Africans—ruler and subject, white man and "nigger," civilized and savage. The British had vested political, economic, and psychological interests in maintaining these contrasts.

The Westernized African was an ever-present reminder to the British that the disparity might be overcome in a single lifetime. They viewed the acculturated African as a threat to their prerogatives and to the established social order. Their response in the literature was to make him a target for ridicule and censure; it was sometimes humorously phrased, but always contemptuous. In Vandeleur's comments on Westernized Liberians, the contempt outweighs the humor.

The Liberian Government is quite a farce; all the members are styled right honourable, but notwithstanding this they have proved quite unable to govern themselves. . . . The Liberians have a very great opinion of themselves and the influence of their state on the affairs of the world, though their knowledge of history is rather vague, as will be gathered from the following story:—A senator met a Frenchman one day in the street, who knocked up against him, when the former in an indignant manner, turned round and said, "You d———Frenchman, what for you shove me? What for we give you at Waterloo?" [36]

A different set of responses were the reiterated emphases on the innate moral and intellectual failings of all Africans, which placed them outside the pale of civilization, if not forever, at least for a very long time. Johnston firmly stated that it would take over three generations for the native Africans to acquire anything approaching a civilized condition, and his was a more modest estimate than many.[37]

At any rate, the quality of African mentality was believed to be of such a nature that any manifestation of civilized behavior was believed to be superficial and tenuous, since sooner or later the African would revert to savagery. Besides, in becoming Westernized, the African could only become corrupted, since his ignorance and immorality always prompted him to adopt Western vices rather than virtues.

We first encounter the widespread use of the term "nigger" during this period. Some writers, like Grogan, saw the Africans only as "niggers"—he used no other term. No issue was taken with the word or its use at this time, though some in positions of administrative responsibility, clearly aware of its pejorative content, eschewed its use. In this connection it is interesting to note that in his earliest writings, Johnston occasionally lapses into using the word, but discreetly, hemmed in by quotation marks.[38] Later, when he became Proconsul of British Empire in Africa, he did not use the term at all.

As for much of the rest of empire-building, the use of "nigger" was borrowed from the Indian Empire. The word was in use there much earlier than in Africa, and the transformation of the Africans to subject peoples equated them in this, as in other aspects, with the Indian subjects. Having already acquired derogatory and tendentious connotations elsewhere, it made a useful label for the new stereotypes and the new image of the Africans.

Fiction of Empire

Surveys of the literature of empire contain bibliographic references to a substantial body of fiction.[1] Many of these novels are still obtainable, and some are still widely read; others have not survived the changing literary tastes and can be obtained only by sustained search.

Novels about Africa had strong appeal for the turn-of-the-century reader. Morton Cohen, the biographer of H. Rider Haggard, suggests that the Victorians were surfeited with the all-too-familiar realities of the domestic novel, and that stirring tales of adventure in exotic locales provided a most welcome change.

For too long the reader's attention had been trained on London slums, prison houses, artists' attics, Manchester mills and village vicarages, and King Solomon's Mines was one of the books that offered a "way out." It let the reader turn his back on the troublesome, the small, the sordid; and it took him on a journey to the Empire's frontier to perform the mighty deeds he could believe in.[2]

In addition, the fiction was generally more exciting than contemporary nonfiction because the novels echoed the thrilling journals of the great period of African exploration at mid-century. Even the few novels of mid-century had been dull reading beside the verve of the explorers' accounts. Novels at the end of the century, however, recaptured that excitement that had been so much a part of the mid-century journals of exploration.

A number of the novels of empire were books for boys. G. A. Henty's *Young Colonists*[3] marched and fought bravely with General Buller to Natal and with General Roberts to Pretoria—glorious scouting adventures, undertaken with high moral purpose and designed to appeal to the young. The battle scenes were described in detail so that a boy might reconstruct the entire encounter with his lead soldiers.[4] Youngsters could readily identify with the young heroes of *Jock of the Bushveld* [5] and *Prester John.*[6]

Sandwiched between incidents of pure adventure were items of deliberate pedagogy: discourses on natural history, British history, and British character. More frequently the instruction was less explicit, but the values were undisguised, presented in high relief. First and foremost, this was a manly literature, relating the deeds of brave men in sport and war, travel, and empire-building. It was, moreover, a highly moral literature which laid great stress on the glorious deeds of idealized British heroes. It was considered by the Victorians to be the right kind of literature for young boys.

These didactic-cum-adventure novels were considered to be of the most elevated moral tone since they were almost entirely sexless in plot. Haggard, for example, guaranteed that in *King Solo-*

mon's Mines "there is not a petticoat in the whole history." [7]
Other novels of this sort do not contain even one feminine character.[8] But there are love stories in others (and we may assume
these were not for boys) in which the romance was either the
central or a peripheral plot, and it was always in terms of the
Victorian ideal: sentimental, moral, and always subordinate to the
adventure.[9]

Often these Victorian novels were highly sexual in overtones
and implications, though conforming superficially to the morality
of the times. *King Solomon's Mines* may have lacked "even a petticoat" but *She* and *Allan Quatermain* quite made up for that lack.
Cohen points out that modern psychological interpretation would
make "Ayesha the projection of Haggard's unconscious idea of the
ideal love . . . and *She* a beautiful allegory of the penalty at-
tendant on our yearning to return into the womb." [10] Repressed
sexuality finds its way into many of these novels by indirection
and innuendo.

Haggard is undoubtedly one of the most significant figures in
the tradition. He assembled into his fiction the greatest number of
themes from the earlier tradition and most directly influenced the
later tradition as well as the fiction of his own period. The Haggard stamp appeared on almost every one of the hundreds of exotic adventure tales that were written after *King Solomon's Mines*.

Bertram Mitford, like Haggard, wrote of the Zulus in the same
blend of pseudo-scholarly and biblical styles, idealizing Zulu chivalry and courage in battle.[11] The Matabele uprisings at the end of
the century provided the background for a number of novels by
Mitford and others.[12] These are all tales of energetic adventure,
but unlike the best of Haggard they lack the quality to capture
the imagination of the modern reader. Their style and content are
dated and of so little interest that now they are forgotten, while
Haggard's most successful novels have become minor classics.

Rudyard Kipling, too, had a pervasive effect on the fiction
about Africa, though he wrote very little about Africa himself.[13]
His few African stories are about the Boer War and contain little
reference to either Africa or the Africans. His African travel essay
is only tangential in pertinence since it deals mainly with his journey in Egypt and along the lower Nile. Yet his stories of the every-

inch-a-Briton, public school, empire-builders in India were models for much fiction about Africa. Edgar Wallace's *Sanders of the River*[14] might have been borrowed directly from Kipling, as might the British officials portrayed in the African novels of Mitford and John Buchan. The "great game" of espionage and international intrigue central to Kipling's *Kim* is also the predominant theme of *Prester John* and *Sanders of the River*.

In his Indian stories, Kipling developed the idea that the colonies were the most admirable school for character building of young Englishmen. This theme was totally taken over by the novelists of Africa. G. A. Henty's *Young Colonists*, the Boy in *Jock of the Bushveld*, young David in *Prester John*, and Drury in *The Fossicker* all emerge from their African ordeals strengthened and ennobled, ready to face the responsibilities of manhood. Allan Quatermain, Sanders, and John Ames demonstrate the characterological virtues of the British gentleman in the face of Africa's challenge.

Africa thus provided the arena and the external stimulus for either the making of man or his destruction. But very few of the Englishmen portrayed in these novels of empire had the fatal character flaws which might entail their destruction. The heroic self-image was too pervasive and the concern with national prestige too great to depict Englishmen who lacked the basic virtues of loyalty, courage, and above all, strong moral fiber. Even in these novels, however, there is the occasional weakling who is destroyed by the African trial, and his failure as a man and an Englishman is even more striking because it is so rare. Yet he, too, serves the same function as the ideal hero, since his failure enhances the hero's success. W. Somerset Maugham's description of such a weakling in *The Explorer* indicates that he could not withstand Africa as a stronger man would.

But the effect of Africa was too strong. Alec had seen many men lose their heads under the influence of that climate. The feelings of authority that seemed so little limited over a race that was manifestly inferior, the subtle magic of the hot sunshine, the vastness, the remoteness from civilization, were very apt to throw a man off his balance. It needed a strong head or a strong morality to avoid the danger, and George had neither. He succumbed.[15]

This sort of character delineation was completely within the Kipling ideal. Kipling's most important influence, however, was not so much in plot or characterization, but as the Bard of Empire. Rhodes was his great hero, and British imperial prestige his great concern. He bitterly denounced the home government during the Boer War only because it had failed to achieve the ideals of his imperial dream; of these ideals he was uncritically jealous. His work was a stentorian paean of praise to the empire which set the tone for the fiction about Africa at the turn of the century and for a long time after.

Maugham's novel *The Explorer* probably survives only because of his later reputation. It is a pretentious and wooden piece, relating the life of Alec Mackenzie, the soldier-explorer par excellence, whose major concern was to "add another fair jewel to England's crown." [16] Stanley was Maugham's avowed model for the super-life-sized hero, but the ideology of the novel was Kipling's. Thus, Alec Mackenzie feels "pride in the great Empire which had sprung from that small island, a greater Rome in a greater world." [17]

The novels of this period were all pro-empire, many actively defending it, others taking it quite for granted. As works of fiction they were free to surround empire with romance, ignore its bitter realities, and invest it with the mystique of the Anglo-Saxon mission to civilize. The British characters understand and willingly shoulder the task of bearing the "white man's burden." In *Prester John*, Buchan simultaneously thrusts maturity and awareness of responsibility upon his young hero.

I knew then the meaning of the white man's duty. He has to take all the risks, recking nothing of his life or his fortunes and well content to find his reward in the fulfillment of his task. That is the difference between white and black . . . the gift of responsibility, the power of being in a little way a king; and so long as we know this and practice it, we will rule not in Africa alone but wherever there are dark men who live only for the day and their own bellies. Moreover the work made me pitiful and kindly. I learned much of the untold grievances of the natives, and saw something of their strange, twisted reasoning.[18]

As in this Buchan novel, justification of the British historic right to dominion and power was usually expressed in terms of racism —the rights and duties of the white man in regard to the inferior blacks. Again it was Kipling who was the leading exponent of this ideology; he firmly believed with his contemporaries, Rhodes and John Ruskin, that only the Anglo-Saxon approached God's ideal type, and that the British were divinely ordained to fulfill the great mission of colonizing Africa.[19]

Olive Schreiner's fiction, especially *The Story of an African Farm*,[20] is, for this period, a literary anomaly, differing in several points from its contemporaries. Neither "manly" literature, adventure, nor a novel of empire, it was the first novel about Africa written by a woman, expressing a feminist viewpoint. In an age of imperialism, the prevailing note of humanitarianism in Schreiner's novel is uncommon. It is, however, a humanitarianism that recalls most sharply the writings of John Barrow and Thomas Pringle in the early nineteenth century. She shared with them a deep compassion for the Africans, and though not actually disapproving of the Boers, she viewed them with a keenly realistic eye. She depicted the inarticulate misery of the African servants on a Boer farm in late nineteenth-century South Africa with pity, but this compassion was only part of her grander ideology of egalitarianism, which was primarily directed to woman's rights. The Africans caught only the sentimental backwash. She perceived very few Africans as individuals; for the most part they are downtrodden, though shadowy, background figures. Schreiner's protest was not so specifically pro-African as it was pro-underdog.

Englishmen did not fare well in Schreiner's book. Of the two that are portrayed, one was an opportunistic scoundrel, and the other a fickle and callow youth. But the English heroine is beautiful, virtuous, kind, and awesomely intellectual. She is the sharpest contrast to the "naked, sullen ill-looking Kaffir woman with lips hideously protruding."[21] Schreiner may have had some revolutionary notions about the status of Victorian women and compassion for the similarly enslaved Negroes, but her basic perception of Africans did not depart from the tradition; she referred to them as "niggers" and held to the traditional conventions concerning their place in nature and society. They were inferior beings whose "race must melt away in the heat of a collision with a higher," and who were "the vestige of one link that spanned between the dog and the white man." [22] Yet it is the general tone of humanitarian protest that Olive Schreiner is remembered for, and in this she was the forerunner of the modern novels of protest concerning race relations in South Africa.

Of all the fiction about Africa written at the turn of the century, only the work of Joseph Conrad stands out as great literature. Conrad wrote but two pieces on Africa: a novella, *Heart of Darkness*, and a short story, "An Outpost of Progress." [23] Both were based on his own experience in the Congo. Though he was one of the major forebears of the twentieth-century tradition, Conrad's influence upon the literature was not apparent until the 1930's; unlike Kipling and Haggard, he had no immediate followers or imitators.

Conrad was also unlike Kipling and Haggard in that he was keenly aware of the moral ambiguities of empire; he was critical of its exploitiveness and profoundly pessimistic about its consequences. He described imperialism as "robbery with violence, aggravated murder on a great scale," and as "conquest of the earth . . . taking it away from those who have a different complexion or slightly flatter noses than ourselves." [24] Yet his indictment was more a condemnation of society than of empire, and his pessimism was directed more toward the inner corruption of mankind than at the evils of colonialism.

Conrad did not abjure the conventions of the imperial tradition in his writing; he was perhaps unaware that he was using them. The Africans seemed to him pitiable, but they were nonetheless "niggers" and "ferocious savages," victimized quite as much by their own stupidity and ignorance as by European brutality. He accepted the mission to civilize as a redeeming "idea and an unselfish belief in the idea," [25] and he idealized the role of the British adventurers and conquerors of Africa as "messengers of the might within the land, bearers of a spark from the sacred fire." [26] He questioned the right and the morality of exploitive colonialism, but he nowhere questioned the superiority of the civilized European, the inferiority of the Africans, nor the British imperial role in Africa.

Conrad's major contribution to the literary tradition was the psychological orientation that is now the mainstay of African novels. Conrad's Africa was the macrocosmic psyche, the very soul of man, the heart of darkness in which the European was compelled to come to terms with himself, there to search out his strengths and weaknesses, to discover the deepest meanings of existence. His journey into Africa was the journey within himself, the penetration of the psyche for self-knowledge. In *Heart of Darkness,* Kurtz's ultimate knowledge was of his own lack of moral resources, and this knowledge spelled his end.

. . . there was something wanting in him . . . whether he knew of this deficiency in himself I can't say. I think the knowledge came to him at last—only at the very last. But the wilderness had found him out early. . . . I think it had whispered to him things about himself which he did not know, things of which he had no conception till he took counsel with the great solitude—and the whisper had proved irresistibly fascinating. It echoed loudly within him because he was hollow at the core.[27]

In a sense Conrad was using the familiar convention—Africa as the testing ground of character—that was typical of the work of his contemporaries. But the convention was transmuted by Conrad; the heart of darkness was Central Africa, but it was also the dark mystery that lay coiled about the very soul of a man.

The fiction at the turn of the century stressed two contrasting and equally important conventions. West Africa was still the fever-ridden white man's grave of the earlier literature, and the novelists wrote of it as the hostile land of darkest mystery. Edgar Wallace said of it, "There are many things that happen in the very heart of Africa that no man can explain . . . a story about Africa must be a mystery story." [28] And Conrad describes the land through the eyes of the two Europeans in "Outpost of Progress."

. . . they felt themselves very much alone, when suddenly left unassisted to face the wilderness; a wilderness rendered more strange, more incomprehensible by the mysterious glimpses of the vigorous life it contained . . . the great silence of the surrounding wilderness, its very hopelessness and savagery seemed to approach them.[29]

There were, however, more novels written about South and East Africa than about the west during this period. They were the areas of greatest imperial concern and of colonial settlement. Here was the vast land of free, open space, where a man might have sufficient room to act out his heroic impulses. England, though the beloved homeland, induced only claustrophobia; it was constraining and drab.

The charm of a life of freedom and complete independence—a life in which a man goes as and where he lists. . . . Not back to the cage. Anything but that! [30]

Already I can hardly bear my impatience when I think of the boundless country and the enchanting freedom. Here one grows so small and mean, but in Africa everything is built to a nobler standard. There the man is really a man. There one knows what are will and strength and courage. You don't know what it is to stand on the edge of some great plain and breathe the pure air. . . .[31]

The novelist was limited by the existing conventions in creating his African setting. Even those totally imaginary locales in the Haggardian novels were sufficiently conventional to seem authentic. Beneath the romantic thriller, the writers wove a strong and intricate web of seeming realism. Readers were often convinced that what they were reading in *King Solomon's Mines* was a true story told by a real person, a white hunter named Allan Quatermain, and the places he told of could be pointed to on the map of Africa.

The self-image of the Briton in the novels paralleled the extravagant contours of his preconceived Africa. He may have come on a quest for health or fortune, for adventure or soldiering, but once in Africa he was bound to establish his own, and British, supremacy. His sphere of action in Africa was the microcosm of empire, and he, on the mission of empire. As in the nonfiction, all the British behaved as if they were personal representatives of Her

Imperial Majesty. Each Briton exemplified his nation's dominance, assured of his acceptance and of his superiority, expecting deference, and demanding it when it was not immediately forthcoming. The British insisted that all Africans defer to them. Mitford's hero, John Ames, makes this point succinctly. "A nigger's a nigger, even if he is high class; all of them should show proper respect to a white man." [32]

The fictional administrators were modeled upon Kipling's Indian administrators—and what men they were!—resourceful, wise, and brave. Each of them knew the natives of his particular district better than they knew themselves, and he governed them with skill, zest, good humor, and even with affection.

Cohen, in his description of Allan Quatermain, has summed up the ideal image of all the British protagonists in this fiction.

The real protagonist is . . . an experienced wise, gentleman . . . an excellent person of unimpeachable honour and genuine feeling. . . . He is clear minded in all situations, prudent, practical, strong-willed, decisive, humble, ingenious, resourceful, sporting, and a devoted friend, a kind master, and of course, an expert rifleman. He gets on with most men very well, regardless of their colour or nationality. . . . But he is an Englishman staunch and steady, and England is his home. He is, in fact, the Englishman of Empire, the Crusader who takes England's divine mission to heart and carries the white man's burden of spreading Christian love and Anglo-Saxon justice to the four corners of the world.[33]

When, in the novels, attention was turned to the Africans, they were seen through the distorting lens of empire. They were always inferior by virtue of their race and their low position on the scale of civilization. The same hallmarks of inferiority that distinguished the beastly savage in the nonfiction of the period were present in the novels.

The term "nigger" appears in all the fiction; the outright imperialists employed the term liberally, but it was so much a part of the contemporary British perception of non-whites that it is even present in the work of Conrad and Schreiner. While it was clearly disparaging, the frequent and almost offhand use of "nigger" leads one to suspect that it was normal usage for all non-whites. And to the British for whom "niggers began at Calais," the term undoubtedly included all non-Anglo-Saxons as well.

The novelists describe the acculturated African with even more distaste than do the writers of nonfiction.

. . . a Sierra Leone nigger . . . spoke English and French with a warbling accent, wrote a beautiful hand . . . and cherished in his innermost heart the worship of evil spirits.[34]

. . . the cheap swagger of the convert to the new civilization.[35]

. . . a Christian Kaffir was an impostor, a bastard and a hypocrite . . . not to be trusted under any circumstances.[36]

Such exaggerated emotional reactions to the Westernized African may have been partially due to the nostalgic trend that was typical of the literature of these times. Often the writers in their "out of the cage" mood conceived of civilization as an insidious poison, corrupting the wild, free Africa and the simple, natural (though savage) African. However, it seems more likely that the issue, in this time of stepped-up empire-building, concerned the Africans as natural subjects rather than as natural men. While the empire-builders might wax sentimentally nostalgic over the game and the land, they could not afford the luxury of being too explicit about the people. Africans bearing any of the trappings of civilization merely confused the issue for the English as portents of things to come. Perhaps, too, they provided a mirror in which the British, however reluctantly, perceived the ambiguities of their self-image and of their entire role in Africa.

The half-caste was as difficult and uncomfortable a by-product of empire as the Westernized African, and the novelists were as censorious of him. There is neither humor nor sympathy in the portrayals, rather a shuddering withdrawal as from something repulsive and disquieting. The "taint of the tar-brush" was a stigma, eliciting the same reaction of hostility as the Westernized African, and for the same reasons. In regard to the half-caste there was an additional factor involving the racist imperative to maintain the purity of blood lines. Miscegenation, besides being immoral, lowered British prestige. Perhaps the major reason for derogation of those of mixed blood was that they muddied the sterling view the British had of themselves. Ernest Glanville describes a half-caste as a "thorough bounder as all of his ilk." [37] Watty, "the half-caste Kaffir lad" in *Fighting the Matabele,* was a braggart, a thief, and most signally a "chicken-hearted fellow"—all of which failings were the direct consequence of hybridization.[38]

In his *Kaffir Stories,*[39] William Charles Scully depicts a half-caste girl whose "Aryan blood told." She was intelligent, loyal, and kind, but she is scarcely an exception to the general trend since "the Aryan element manifested itself mainly in force of character and ability; for in her tastes and desires, as in her physiognomy, she followed her mother's race." In the end, of course, her "African blood" won out; she ran off with her African lover and lived and died in the bush with him. Thus the bloodlines maintain their integrity, and racism provides the answer.

Scully's book is one of the few novels of this period in which Africans have more than a minor role. Highly conventional in all other aspects, in this regard at least, *Kaffir Stories* broke some new ground. Haggard, following the pattern set earlier by Stanley and Thomson in their "all-African" novels, wrote *Nada the Lily,*[40] in which all the characters are African. Scully's Africans were stereotyped, but placed in a realistic context; Haggard's Zulus in *Nada the Lily* were noble savages in never-never land. Published in 1892, *Nada the Lily* is anachronistic in its harking back to the noble savages of mid-nineteenth-century fiction. This is not a convention which is typical of or congenial to the fiction of empire.

Turn-of-the-century approximations of the noble savage were stereotyped depictions of "loyal" savages or "warriors." They were viewed with sympathy and even liking, but described in terms of the single dominant and traditionally phrased quality. The "loyal" Africans were the very best of subject peoples and they were described with humor and affection. Gert, the Hottentot hunter and servant in *The Fossicker,* is distinguishable from Khiva, the Zulu guide in *King Solomon's Mines,* and Pukele, the Matabele gunboy in *John Ames,* only by details of dress and appearance; their characters are almost identical. All were keen fighters, trackers, and faithful to the death to their white masters, whom they died defending. In such cases, the only noble savage obviously had to be a dead one!

An even clearer echo of the noble-savage romance is the idealized portrayal of Zulu warriors. Admiration for the Zulu seemed almost mandatory for the novelists of empire.

Like all Zulus, the aristocrats of the native tribes, they were lithe and well-formed, with the stamp of war upon their faces. Their intense pride of birth and contempt for all others were visible in the poise of their heads and their dignified bearing.[41]

Jim was one of the real fighting Zulu breed . . . and they were always ready for a fight and would tackle any odds when their blood was up.[42]

And now, behold, Umslopogaas, I know thee for a great warrior of the blood royal, faithful to the death. Even in Zulu land, where all men are brave, they called thee "the Slaughterer," and at night told stories round the fire of thy strength and deeds.[43]

Although the British identified with and admired the brave, warlike Zulus, they qualified their admiration by depicting them also as the wildest of savages, uncontrollable berserkers, lacking any restraint when their blood lust was roused, ". . . the savage with all self-control flung to the winds." [44] Haggard said that when the Zulu was roused "he is like a fiend." [45] In this regard the Zulu personified the complete contrast to what was probably the most highly valued British trait, the restraint of aggressive impulse.

The warrior who displayed physical courage, loyalty, and who fought fairly was an exemplar of the British code of honor. These same values were projected onto certain of the domestic animals in the novels. *Jock of the Bushveld* is an eponymous tale of a noble hunting dog who personified all the virtues attributed to the Zulu and to the British themselves. He possessed the qualities of "courage, fidelity and concentration" that marked nobility of character. In the same novel there is an exceedingly virtuous horse.

Tsetse was also an old soldier, but he was what you might call a gentleman old soldier, with a sense of duty; and in his case the discipline and honour of his calling were not garments for the occasion, but part of himself.[46]

Apparently the British did not require human intellect to achieve the status of gentleman or soldier. The noble animals served a distinct and unique literary function, for in addition to personifying British virtue, the writers projected onto them an overt hostility toward the Africans that they would not and could not admit of themselves. As dedicated "Crusaders" of empire, the British were to help, to educate, even to fight the Africans, but never to exhibit hatred. A true gentleman could openly admit only to feelings of protectiveness and affection for his savage charges, but his dogs (also gentlemen) instinctively hated them, and lacking the human qualities of self-control, exhibited hostility by growling, barking, and openly attacking Africans.

In general, the novels of empire expressed the British devotion to country and dedication to the civilizing mission in Africa. They expressed as well the characterological virtues which reflected British values. In these respects they were similar to and supported the contemporaneous nonfiction. Nor did the major themes of the novels differ from those of the factual accounts; in both the descriptions of the land, sport, beasts, and people were the same. Where the novels differ from the nonfiction was in affording greater literary freedom to elaborate on the mystique of Africa and to proliferate all the images. Most significantly, the fictional embellishments presented even more dramatically the case for empire.

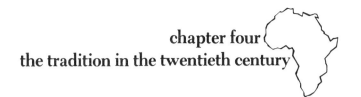

THE British Empire in Africa, so arduously acquired in the nineteenth century, was lost in the twentieth. The Boer War (1899–1902) marked both the apogee of the empire in Africa and the beginning of its decline. It resulted in the consolidation of large and desirable territories, but at the same time it exposed crucial areas of weakness. The mere fact that so much time, effort, men, and materiel had to be expended in the "little war with the Boer Republics"[1] weakened British prestige and self-confidence. This, the first in a series of White Men's wars fought on African soil, disrupted the united white front which had, however tenuously, been maintained throughout the partitioning of Africa.

World War I, demonstrating how tenuous the united front had been, hastened the decline of African colonialism. The postwar fate of the German colonies was a portent: it was the first European empire in Africa to end. Outright imperialism yielded to mandated trusteeship. The British policy of the Dual Mandate had always assumed responsibility for the welfare of subject peoples, but the newer principle committed the European trustees, at least in theory, to foster African self-determination. Italy's invasion of Abyssinia in 1935 ran sufficiently counter to the new concepts so that the League of Nations invoked sanctions. Empire-building was now deemed aggression, rather than the expression of "manifest destiny," and the whole idea of empire was in bad odor.

Economic crisis and social unrest marked the period between the two world wars. The spread of Marxist thought and the rise of fascism were responses to the difficult times and both were hostile to Great Britain's imperial rule. Ideological attacks on the empire,

Britain's own economic plight, and unrest within the colonies, particularly in India, further diminished British faith in empire.

The rise of Nazi Germany involved Great Britain in a second world war. The challenge of nazism had to be met, and Great Britain responded to totalitarianism by reaffirming liberal, democratic values. Racism, always opposed by humanitarians, had to be refuted as the ideology of the enemy. Modern science had exposed the fallacies of racism, and scientific opinions were now publicized to discredit Nazi propaganda.[2] Racism joined imperialism and jingoism as obsolescent ideologies.

The years between 1910 and 1960 saw radical change on the continent of Africa as well. Roads, railways, airports and modern communications linked regions within Africa and Africa with the world. New knowledge and techniques in medicine and hygiene attacked the problems of disease. Industrial developments led to concentrations of population, creating an increasingly urban mode of life. The new African elite, trained and educated by the West, was impatient with colonial status and anxious to test its new powers. It was from this group that new political leaders arose, to spearhead movements for national independence. Great Britain, impoverished by two world wars, her imperial impulse spent, could not or would not summon the force to retain colonies that demanded sovereignty. Beginning with Ghana in 1957, one by one the African colonies were granted independence. In the short time span since the Berlin Conference in 1884, the status of Africa underwent a remarkable change: from booty to be parceled out among the European powers it became a land of sovereign nations.

The literature of the first decades of the twentieth century lagged behind the events. The British still wrote as if Africa were a colonial possession which they held in the full confidence that this state of affairs would go on forever. And, indeed, in the early years of the century the surface of British-African relations seemed undisturbed. In this period of relative quiescence the literary conventions and stereotypes formulated during the height of empire became the fixed pattern for all the literature to follow.

The long careers of certain writers form the most obvious link with the literature of the past. Sir Harry Johnston began his work with the account of his exploration of the Congo in 1884 and ended it almost fifty volumes later with the publication of *The Story of My Life* in 1923. Lugard's writings dated from *The Rise of Our East African Empire* in 1883 to 1945, when his last articles appeared. For both of these architects of empire little seemed to have changed. Their later works are entirely consistent with their earlier.

Time stood still as well for novelists like John Buchan and Edgar Wallace, who wrote from before World War I until the 1930's. During twenty-one years of service Wallace's hero, District Officer Sanders, achieved the rank of Commissioner and managed to learn the drum language, a skill that as a young officer he had considered impossible for a white man. That is the sum and substance of change in Wallace's novels. Buchan, too, depicts Africans in 1936 almost exactly in the same terms that he did in 1910.

I heard a sound which I had not heard since the Matabele Rising, the deep throaty howl of Kaffirs on the war-path . . . this outrage of their sacred place had awakened their manhood. Once they had been a famous fighting clan and the old fury had revived. . . . Also there were scores of them, the better part of a hundred lusty savages, mad with fury at the violation of their shrine.[3]

. . . a mob of maddened savages surged around me. They were chanting a wild song and brandishing spears and rifles to its accompaniment. From their bloodshot eyes stood the lust of blood, the fury of conquest—all the aboriginal passions . . . a wave of black savagery seemed to close over my head.[4]

The twentieth-century biographers of the builders of empire do not discredit either the empire or its architects. For the most part they are in sympathy, if not full agreement, with their subjects. Their accounts reiterate their heroism and idealism as well as the imperial view of Africa.[5]

The proconsuls of empire, Lugard and Johnston, have a long line of literary descendants, some as recent as 1958. Whether journal or memoir, accounts by government officials in Africa are in the Lugard-Johnston vein. There are few differences in basic attitudes, perceptions, and concepts, but changed conditions of work and travel modify the narratives. Modern transport, for example, obviates the long, often exasperated, chapters devoted to organization and conduct of the safari. Capture of Mau Mau leaders—facilitated by jeeps, planes, and bombs[6]—makes an altogether different story from the military actions in the nineteenth century. British courage never goes out of style, but modern opportunities for its exercise are diminished.

The improved communications made for greater administrative efficiency. The price of efficiency was, however, often seen as the loss of independence, self-reliance, and individuality. The modern British colonial officer was, however reluctantly, a bureaucrat and had little of the rugged individualism of the empire-builders which often led one to wonder whether they were agent or incarnation of England. The outstanding difference is that the early officials were writing of the job to be done, and the later officials discuss its accomplishment. The former presented the case for empire, making commitments and justifying their plans and activities; the latter defend the programs, stating that, in retrospect the commitments had been fulfilled and the empire vindicated. Sir Charles Dundas, former Governor of Uganda and colonial official of long experience, writes.

Today the word Empire is taboo; we may not speak of subject races, they have become backward peoples; colonial rule has become "trusteeship." . . . A chapter of world history has therewith been closed. Whether another chapter of comparable benefits to the human race will be written may be questioned. Certainly more was done for backward mankind in the era of British colonial rule than in any previous age, and if colonialism is now discredited I believe that its passing will nevertheless be mourned by the simple people of one-time British colonies as the end of a Golden Age.[7]

All the autobiographies, whether or not directly concerned with colonial administration, uphold the values and concepts of imperialism and consequently project the standard images. It is perhaps natural that those who wrote about empire should write in the idiom of empire. What is more significant is that this idiom should have dominated so many other writers on Africa. Traders, settlers, prospectors, and tourists tended to be equally imperialist in sentiment. It is as if the nineteenth century never ended for them, for they cling to the Kipling notion of the "little brown brother" even though they may have given up hope of empire along with the solar topee.

The production of novels placed in an African setting increased markedly after the turn of the century. The bibliography of the period since 1910 contains approximately four times as many works of fiction as that of the entire preceding three hundred and fifty years. Like the nonfiction, the novels and short stories have their prototypes in the earlier literature—namely in the work of Haggard, Conrad, and Kipling.

The themes of the modern fiction fall into two major categories: one emphasizes action and the quest for adventure; the other stresses psychology and the quest for identity. In contemporary writing some interweaving of these themes is fairly common. Tales of the encounters between dauntless heroes and ferocious beasts or savage natives were more typical of the first decades of the century. The simple adventure novel is now out of date; adventure must be weighted with introspection. However, neither the adventure nor the introspection stray very far from the lines laid out by Conrad and Haggard.

The works of Conrad and Haggard are not only prototypes; they have been incorporated into the mystique of Africa. It has become standard literary practice to cite them as if the mention of their names added authenticity and heightened effect to the account. Haggard is regularly invoked as if he were a minor deity, and some writers, Peter Viertel, for example, create the appropriate atmosphere by summoning Conrad.

When he said "Africa" he seemed to give the word a greater meaning than it had ever had for me. . . . I had the spontaneous feeling of darkness and evil. Everything Conrad had said in thousands of words about the black, stagnant river where Kurtz had died was echoed in Wilson's pronunciation of the name of that continent. I saw twisted trees and jungles and black rivers. . . .[8]

Kipling is not explicitly invoked because he is out of fashion as a writer and because, having written little about Africa, he is not identified with Africa. His stories of the empire in India, however, remain as prototypes for African novels in which colonial administration is the dominant theme and the administrators the major characters. The recent novel *Jimmy Riddle*, by Ian Brook, follows the Kipling model so closely that the band of clever young colonial officials might have stepped right out of *Stalky & Co.*

Joyce Cary is probably the most significant of the twentieth-century British novelists to write about Africa. In view of the low esteem in which Kipling has been held, it may seem like heresy to link Cary to him. But not only are their writings similar in theme and content, they also share to some extent a commitment to empire and a serious concern with its problems. In writing of empire as the arena for the interplay of moral forces, both authors emerge as idealists, advocates of moral purpose rather than power politics. They are sensitive to the ambiguities inherent in British morality and values, to the clash of cultures in the imperial venture and its reflections in human expenditure. Of course, Cary is a modern; his patriotism is muted, his tone ironic, and he shrills no clarion call for empire. Cary, unlike Kipling, is totally lacking in racism. None of his characters can be comfortably categorized as Negro or white, civilized or savage. Every one is a highly idiosyncratic individual. Yet, his portrayals of individuals, African and European, are built out of the traditional conventions by a process of subtle selection.

Cary is not an uncritical advocate of colonialism. He makes his position explicit in his nonfictional work, *The Case for African Freedom*. Scarcely what its title indicates, this book does not support African independence. It is a critique of British colonial administration and a plea for reform and a more enlightened policy.

Certain of the twentieth-century novels are truly anticolonial.[9] Winifred Holtby, Evelyn Waugh, and Gwyn Griffin attack the whole notion of British competence to rule. But even in these novels the portrayal of Africans is entirely conventional. Anticolonialism has little effect on their depiction of Africa and the Africans, for they tend to stress the futility of the attempt to civilize savages. These novelists direct their criticism at the decadence of British culture, and anticolonialism becomes the vehicle by which they express their discontent with the state of the modern world.

A distinct genre of fiction of social protest exists in modern novels of South Africa. The works of Doris Lessing, Nadine Gordimer, Alan Paton, and Dan Jacobson represent some of the most distinguished and widely read fiction about Africa. They exhibit a slight family resemblance to the earlier work of Olive Schreiner in their prevailing humanitarian and egalitarian outlook. Their egalitarianism, however, belongs to the twentieth century and is explicitly antiracist and anti-imperialist. These novels seem irrelevant to a discussion of the British literary tradition about Africa because they are concerned with problems of the multiracial society and not with the image of Africa or the British in Africa.

Doubt and disillusion predominate in much of the recent literature, and they are usually expressed quite apart from any reference to colonialism or race relations. The writers have shifted from the domain of social problems and public issues to the narrower sphere of the individual and his psyche.

Whether the literary approach is based upon the Victorian certainties or upon modern uncertainties, the formal aspects of the tradition are constant. The stereotypes and idioms may have undergone some evaluative revisions, but they remain as the same contrastive conventions. The narrative still emphasizes the confrontation of civilized values with their savage negation.

As fashions in attitudes have changed at least some of the details in the tradition have changed too. Growing secularism has outmoded any concern with the African as "heathen." The Africans are no longer described as ugly, a frequent judgment during the more parochial nineteenth century. A new sophistication has led to appreciation of the beauty of exotic people, and the Africans have come in for their share of admiration.

In general there is an increased awareness of cultural variation among the Africans manifested in frequent and accurate use of ethnographic detail. In a sense the literature reflects the coming of age of anthropology, since the authors pride themselves on the authenticity of their descriptions of tribal customs and history. But modern anthropology only adds detail to the fundamental conceptions which remain traditional.

Alan Scholefield's recent novels about South Africa in the early nineteenth century [10] are precise in their ethnography and history, as well as meticulously preserving the feeling and ethos of the period. The very vocabulary of his characters evokes the time and place with economy and elegance. But the characters themselves are stock figures, familiar through long acquaintance. We meet again the "loyal Bushman boy," first encountered in Pringle, the Zulu berserker, obviously kin to Haggard's Umslopogaas, as well as a duplicate of his venomous old hag who smells out witches. The European characters are also old friends: the young Scottish protagonist seeking his fortune ever deeper in the interior, at peace only away from civilization; the humane old doctor whose passion is specimen-collecting; survivors from the wreck of the *Grosvenor;* and Boers, some patriarchal and others brutal.

Scholefield's novels demonstrate the literary value of the tradition which provides the ingredients for lively novels: the stock characters are nevertheless striking figures, the incidents are exciting, and the setting colorful. In contrast there are some recent novels that have bypassed the tradition. That they are set in Africa is a matter of geographical interest only. Eric Ambler's recent thriller, for example, and a few detective stories are set in an Africa without mystique and incidentally without much interest.[11] In view of the lackluster Africa of the tradition-free novels it is not surprising that writers continue to mine the accumulated riches of the tradition.

Continued conformity to the tradition is not without its problems. Contemporary disapproval of racism forces some alteration in twentieth-century writing. Outright racist ideas are scarcely respectable, and the writers avoid their direct statement. Since they are governed by the tradition, however, they are constrained, despite themselves, to racist evaluations. The authors try to avoid racism while conforming to the conventions by feats of literary gymnastics. For example, Dr. Grantly Dick Read's attempt to combine science and the tradition seems erudite on the surface, but science is defeated by the conventional racial determinism.

. . . but we must accept again the argument that although environment is one of the strongest influences in the development of the mind, it can never supplant or change the fundamental characteristics of an individual. The environment of the "cultured" European is entirely different from the hereditary environment of the African, but the genetic constitutions of the two peoples remain unaltered.[12]

In attempts to resolve the dilemma caused by the discrepancy between the new attitudes toward race and the exigencies of the literary tradition, authors cite hearsay and anonymous authorities. Stuart Cloete's "doctor" is nameless, but under the guise of scientific authority he provides the writer with seeming validation of the old racist stereotypes.

I had an interesting talk with the doctor who has been eight years in the Congo, about some of the differences between the white man and the black. . . . Actually the differences have not been sufficiently studied, but some believe that the brain and nervous system are as different as the body and organs from those of the white man. This would suggest that the African's development would follow different lines even if he becomes Westernized. The doctor considered that the tribal Africans were satisfied with eating, breeding, fighting and dancing.[13]

Belief in Social Darwinism as explanation of British superiority has collided with the newer doctrines of psychoanalysis. Freud also assumed evolutionary stages of human society, but cast doubts upon the idea that civilization and progress are unequivocally worthwhile. Victorian morality is transmuted into unwholesome repression, religious faith into an illusion, and civilization is marked more by discontent than satisfaction. The literature on Africa translates these concepts into a neo-primitivism that stands the conventions on their heads. The savage African is simple and content, close to nature and the eternal verities. Progress has led only to the destruction of essential human values. The British still find themselves at the top of the evolutionary ladder, but their position there is rapidly becoming unbearable. These concepts have influenced the current shift from social and political issues to psychological concerns. The thread of psychoanalysis which runs through modern writing on Africa is the new significant element in the tradition.

The twentieth-century modifications of the tradition can scarcely be described as revolutionary. They do not alter the basic images of Africa. The most striking feature of all the literature is still the continuity within its governing tradition. The influence of nineteenth-century writing seems to have so shaped concept and preconception of Africa that even the innovations of new ideologies and of highly creative writers are but further elaborations of the tradition rather than departures from it.

By far the most significant development of the tradition in the twentieth century is its formalization. All the elements of the tradition as it appears in current writing were present in the literature of the nineteenth century. Yet the conventions, metaphors, and stereotypes used to describe Africa, the Africans, and the British were unstructured and diffuse. All these separate elements coalesced to become the highly complex and integrated series of images that dominate the twentieth-century literature.

The chapters which follow present an analysis of these images and their interrelations. Each image in the series expresses only one aspect of the total contrast between Africa and England and between the Africans and the English. Each image, however, is an entity in its own right. The depiction of the continent as the setting for the narrative is usually the first and most obvious indication of the particular image the author will establish. It seems expedient, then, to categorize the entire image by the metaphor describing the continent.

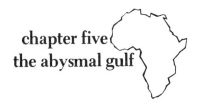

THE fundamental theme in twentieth-century British writing about Africa is that Africa constitutes a world apart. All its features—the land itself, the people, the animals, and the vegetation—are viewed as too alien to be encompassed within the normal rubrics of civilized understanding. Exaggerations of the differences between Africa and Europe make the two continents appear entirely discrete phenomena, lacking any similarity or continuity. Attempted explanations of the cause for this disparity attribute to Africa a unique geology, biology, human history and, indeed, a unique soul. Europe and Africa are envisioned as separate worlds with a deep and abiding gulf between them, and their differences are so irreconcilable that the gulf can never be bridged.

The conventions of this image of the continent focus upon its great antiquity, its formidable size, and its resistance to domestication. These qualities make the essential contrast. Ancient, vast, and wild, Africa is the opposite of small, cozy, industrialized England. These are, to be sure, old and familiar elements of the tradition which now become preconditions for the modern attitude that the Briton is out of his element in Africa. He is intimidated by the foreboding that he and his works will be annihilated.

The notion of Africa's great age recurs in a variety of phrasings and as part of several of the images. The land, the people, the fauna, and the flora are presumed to be relics of some remote era. In this image of the Gulf the convention reinforces the singularity of Africa; no other continent is so old.

Geologically the shield of Africa is old, but not older than other continental shields. The ancient shield of Canada produces literary clichés about Canada's lusty youth. Obviously geological dating has little relevance to the chronology assigned by literary traditions. In fact, geology, like other sciences, simply provides grist for the mill of literary metaphor.

. . . I begin with the earth of Africa. Now, Africa is old in the longest measure of time on earth. It is old in a way which makes the lovely white mountains in Switzerland not solid immovable matter but waves curling and breaking in the storm of time, wherein even Everest is but the ghostly spume of spray torn by an angry gust from curling breakers. Long before vegetable, organic, or biological matter were in being, the rocks and earth of Africa as we know them today were already formed.[1]

In this passage, Laurens Van der Post grants Africa an inordinately great age and further implies that it has remained throughout time as it was at the beginning. Africa is thus not only old, but unchanging as well. For the modern writer, Max Catto, as it was for Sir Harry Johnston, Africa is a time machine by which to enter the world of antiquity.

It was all as primitive as the brontosaurus. Life swarmed savagely and voraciously down there, as nakedly ravenous as in those past ages when Africa was formed. . . . "—Go into that forest, I'm telling you, it's like walking back into the beginning of the world."[2]

A world that has endured without change for countless ages does not yield readily to any attempt at alteration. There is a refrain throughout the writing that the British in Africa are out of place and time, temporary intruders, unable to make even a small imprint to mark their passage. Richard Wyndham recounts, "I felt for the first time the fear which a civilized being must experience in a landscape that has not changed since the world began."[3]

Africa's great size, quite real enough, is overstressed in the literature. This exaggeration of size bolsters the idea that it is an unchanging and unyielding land; sheer mass overwhelms man's efforts and sheer space dwarfs him and his ambitious schemes to insignificance. Elspeth Huxley in the following passage seems to have further augmented the oppressive size of Africa by adding to it the Indian Ocean and even India.

. . . Robert . . . stared into the darkness that concealed the vast interior. A hundred, a thousand miles and more it stretched, bush and jungle and desert, away beyond imagination to the swamps of Chad, to forests of the Congo, beyond that again to the headwaters of the Nile, the Mountains of the Moon and the land of the lakes, to reach that ocean which lapped the Indian shore. Confronted with such immensity, his irritation seemed petty, even the elation of the morning absurd. How could one man's foot shake the earth of such a continent.[4]

Vast and ancient, Africa seems impervious to the most strenuous British efforts; it will not permit any inroads of their civilization. Reflecting twentieth-century political changes, the British now write of their feelings of transiency, intimidated by the land over which they had formerly been the confident masters. They see themselves not as conquerors but as trespassers on the alien continent. Many writers echo Lady Packer's cry, "This isn't our place."[5]

The image follows through to its logical culmination; British entry into Africa was fruitless. The gulf is too great, and attempts to bridge it are futile. The artifacts of civilization—buildings, roads, bridges—everything will be obliterated, for they are ephemeral in the face of Africa's permanence.

Conquerors have come and gone. Africa has swallowed them.[6]

How soon would . . . western civilization be devoured by the atavism of the Dark Continent?[7]

Do you realize that quite soon *we* shall be the past? And what will there be to show that we have ever existed? We shall be swallowed up like everything else in a dreadful, sunny limbo.[8]

The land wore these flashy gew-gaws of civilization slightly askew like a comic mask which was always falling down, cracking up, the plaster splitting as the ants and the sun and the roots of the palms and the baobabs and the acacias pushed and ate and gnawed and nagged away at this little pancake of the Western world.[9]

Africa has negated the very spirit of British progress. The optimism of the empire-builders is gone. The British protagonist seems defeated almost before he starts in his attempts to pit himself against the unyielding perdurance of Africa. All the energy, all the will toward change that he brings with him from Britain cannot prevail against the immutability of the Dark Continent. He feels a boundless frustration in his encounter with "that enormous reserve of inertia with which . . . Ethiopia confounds Europe." [10]

The population of Africa, across the fathomless abyss, is as antithetical to the English as the continent itself is to England. The Africans are too alien, too different even to be understood. Their languages, their cultures, their mentality belong to an entirely different order of humanity. No Englishman, despite long residence in Africa and close contact with the people, can hope to comprehend them. Those who believe they do understand the Africans are deluding themselves, for the core of African character is so enigmatic that it is simply unintelligible to the European. Statements to this effect occur in almost every modern book on Africa.

If the Africans are a mystery to the British, the British are equally inexplicable to the Africans. According to John Rowan Wilson, for example, they find the British utterly bewildering and understand nothing of their behavior or their point of view.

He was a phenomenon totally incomprehensible to them . . . what can he have represented to men to whom the last 2,000 years, which had produced him, were totally unknown? They could not dispute with him. When he tried to explain what he was doing, they stood before him, understanding nothing. . . . There was no judgement available to them but that of their emotions, primitive, amorphous; no weapon but that of force. . . .[11]

The literature frequently alleges that the very thought processes of the African and the British are of a different nature. There are solemn discussions which describe the "round mind" of the Africans, proferring as evidence their predilection for the curved line —round houses, curvilinear designs, winding pathways, and irregular plowing. Numerous statements aver that Africans are unable to do anything in a straight line, and this is interpreted as indicative of the strangeness and inferiority of African mentality.

Because of his "round mind" the African is forever barred from attaining full participation in straightforward, right-thinking Western civilization.

Culturally determined motor habits and styles are thus defined as innate inadequacies. In reality, not all Africans are biased in favor of curved lines. In West and Central Africa the houses are rectangular, and straight-line designs are common. The problem, in any case, is not one of the "African mind," but rather refers to a cultural tradition which conditions the manner of all perception and execution.

The writers ignore the factors of cultural conditioning. They base the lack of mutual understanding on the accepted myths of immutable inherited characteristics. Their facile reliance upon heredity indicates that biological determinism is still a bedrock of the twentieth-century tradition. Culture, character, and temperament are still taken to be inherent traits carried in the "blood." Anything from craftsmanship to violence to superstition can, at the author's discretion, be attributed to the blood line. Augustus Collodon's statement on the genetics of cannibalism differs from the similar statements of others only in its blatant absurdity.

These two boys came from cannibal stock. In their blood was the hereditary taint that no civilization or education could eradicate. When a cannibal instinct came to the surface, we were shocked, horrified, disgusted and revengeful—but really the fault was our own. If we had treated them all along as cannibals we would have known what to expect. It was because we ourselves invested them with a higher-than-cannibal mentality that they disappointed us so dreadfully. . . . You can't turn a horse into a camel.[12]

Apparently "blood" is not only a cause, it is the only cause. Cultural conditioning, life-experience, and sheer chance count for little. Despite the widespread interest in psychology, there seems no need to refer to any of the other factors that shape personality. The highly individuated psyches of the Europeans often receive a rather tender regard. The Africans, however, share a tribal psyche, and the conventional stereotypes of tribe and race suffice to portray and to explain the individual. Membership in a tribe confers upon the individual his talents, virtues, and vices; his

leaders—men of unquestioned loyalty, courage, and discipline—the products of a ruling class born and bred to its position. Then Great Britain was ruled by gentlemen, and Great Britain ruled the world.

Class stability and privilege and national power are inextricably bound together in this picture of the past. In the African colonies this ideal social and political order was epitomized, clear-cut, and intact: there was no blurring of the social hierarchy; the British were masters, the Africans subjects. To those British for whom the modern situation spells impoverishment and an unwonted loss of prestige, Africa, by virtue of the anachronism of the image, still holds the promise of retention of their status. The contemporary novelist Gwyn Griffin underlines the overwhelming value of this promise to the new poor.

Like most of their class their lives were spent in contriving somehow, to hold on at least the outward appearance of their social position, and their greatest fear . . . of forfeiting their precious gentility. . . . It is inevitably such people who, as young men go out to fill the most thankless positions in the least attractive of British colonial territories in the knowledge that however questionable their social situation in England, once they are east of Suez they will habitually be addressed as "lord"—even if only in exotic synonyms of "sahib," "bwana," or "tuan." Out they come, pinkfaced, pink-kneed, pathetically eager to hunt big game, trek endlessly through vast open spaces, rule savage tribes. Out they come as assistant district commissioners, assistant superintendents of police, second-lieutenants of third-rate native levies, or junior overseers on plantations of a dozen varieties of tropical produce. For such occupations are generally considered to offer "a gentleman's life" and most of those who undertake them, would, perhaps, accept the job of shoveling coal in hell if they believed it to do the same.[11]

Africa appears as the special preserve of the British upper classes. The colonial administrators and settlers, even the transient visitors, are distinguished for their blue blood, their old school ties, and a predilection for the outdoor life, especially for the more active, violent sports. Such men were considered the fit rulers of empire. In his foreword to H. M. Jackson's work on the Sudan, Lord Vansittart extols their qualifications.

I have never wavered in my conviction that the Sudan Civil Service was the finest body in the world. . . . They were all picked men, scholars and athletes. . . . Look at their credentials! A former Rugby football captain of Oxford and Scotland, an ex-captain of the Cambridge University soccer XI, a racing trials man, [etc.]. . . . This was a typical intake, chosen not by examination but by shrewd judges of capacity not only to survive in but to administer huge wild districts. Entrance went by character and the strength to bear early responsibility. These traits are typical of the British at their best.[12]

Memoirs of the "old Africa hands," as well as modern accounts, make very clear the satisfactions of British life in Africa. They concentrate on its freedoms, opportunities for sport and companionship, the plentiful, cheap servants, and they discount the difficulties of climate and isolation. In short, the life of the colonial officer and settler was an idealized counterpart of British county life in the "good old days." Lord Cranworth recalls the luxury, so inexpensively procured, of his African estate.

We spent some of the happiest years of our lives at Chiromo, and never before or since have I been so rich. We had the best car in the Protectorate, the best civilian house, three ponies and a goat carriage, a first-class Goan cook . . . a spacious and most beautiful garden, and syces, domestic servants, and gardeners without stint. Our total expenditures on these was about £1200 a year.[13]

This literature of reminiscence is a valedictory to empire that stresses the unselfish motives of the British. Their dedication to the ideals of responsible service outweighed any desire for self or class aggrandizement. Just as the picture of good living is an important facet of the literature, even more is the depiction of devoted and arduous labor.

The valedictory to empire is made with a clear conscience; the zeal, the devotion, and the self-sacrifice were justified by their results. In short, it was "a golden age," but according to the literature it was as much the golden age for the British in Africa as for the Africans.

The African is depicted as the willing and grateful recipient of British beneficence. He is a child—not the child of nature as in the image of primal Africa—but the untutored child in the nursery. He is by nature subservient and responsive to a kind, but firm regime. The relationship between Briton and African resembles that between parent and child. Any coercion used in dealing with the Africans was not aggression; it was, rather, akin to the discipline of children—for their own welfare. A. C. G. Hastings, a former colonial official, phrases it as being administered in the "spirit of correction and eventual good." [14] As children ought to do, the Africans accepted just correction from authority without resentment. The British sentiment that force does not vitiate benevolence is presumably established by the reports of African loyalty, trust, respect, and even love for their British masters. The British mandate to rule was thus validated by African acceptance.

The loyal African servant is a stock figure in both fiction and nonfiction. Whatever faults he may have are redeemed by his devotion to his master. That this should be an overriding virtue reflects the British (or perhaps human) desire for love and approbation. The loyal servants, however, are significant figures, for they are the only Africans who elicit love from the British. This love seems the only bridge to span the gulf. Haggard writes that it even reaches beyond the grave.

Or if my Mazook should be dead, and if there is any future for us mortals, and if Zulus and white men go to the same place—as why should they not?—then I am quite certain that when I reach that shore I shall see a square-faced, dusky figure seated on it, and hear the words, "Inkoos Indanda, here am I, Mazook, who once was your man, waiting to serve you." For such is the nature of the poor despised Zulu, at any rate towards one whom he may choose to love.[15]

For some writers the "Golden Age" preserved in the Land in Amber is medieval Europe rather than Eden or empire. Feudalism represents a social order in which an individual was secure in his identity and his social role. Furthermore, it permitted a gentleman by birth and by breeding to live by the code of honor. A number of writers attempt to recapture that chivalry long lost in Britain by projecting it onto Africa and certain groups of Africans. Dinesen, thus, makes a true "gentleman" out of her Somali servant, Farah, along with the Somalis in general.

In our day the word "gentleman" is taken less seriously than before.
. . . If the word may be taken to describe or define the person who has
got the code of honour of his period and milieu in his own blood, as
an instinct—such as the rules of the game will be in the blood of the
true cricket or football player to whom it would not be possible in
any situation to throw the ball at the head of his adversary—Farah
was the greatest gentleman I have ever met.[16]

The idealization of feudalism in this literature carries with it an
idealization of warfare. Final validation of oneself as a man and a
gentleman is achieved primarily through combat, for the chivalric
code of honor is essentially a warrior's code. Warfare is a completely masculine activity by which a man can absolutely validate
his manhood. Sheer physical courage—the willingness to face
death in battle—is the essential virtue.

Modern civilization is decried because it lacks an equally ready
definition of a masculine ideal. The incredibly destructive and de-
humanized nature of modern warfare renders the older ideal of
the gallant warrior meaningless. With increased mechanization
there is opportunity for neither gallantry nor honor, and the
bonds of good fellowship are replaced by the bonds of shared
misery and fear. The writers turn from this reality to glorify the
warrior who fought like a man and died a hero.

The ideal of manliness, exemplified in the warrior, transcends
differences in race, language, and culture. The writers are still
ready, along with Kipling, to "give the certifikit" to the "Poor be-
nighted 'eathen who's a first class fighting man." The mystique of
the warrior culminates in the almost worshipful British attitude
toward the Masai. Some officials became so enamored of the
Masai that their administrative effectiveness was impaired. It occurred often enough to be designated as the disease of "masaitis,"
and those infected with it were transferred to other posts. "Masaitis" is not limited to colonial officialdom; it permeates the modern literature. Respect for the Masai is mandatory, even if the
author has had no more than the routine tourist glimpse of them.
Grantly Dick Read implies that recognition of the worth of the
Masai can serve as an index of the worthiness of the British. "We
clearly understood why the best type of white man holds them in
such high esteem and even real affection." [17]

One can understand the cult of Masai worship only by recognizing that the bases of British perception rest upon a concept of aristocracy partly defined in terms of feudal values and partly in those of nineteenth-century gentry. Aristocracy becomes associated with a somewhat curious syndrome of traits: disdain for the tradesman, impassioned interest in domestic animals, appreciation of the value of pedigree for man and beast, disciplined self-possession as well as marked self-assurance, and above all, a chivalric preoccupation with warfare.

British adulation of the Masai is based on their seemingly upper-class attitudes. The Masai do little work, aside from tending the herds (and even here much of the labor is done by boys). They generally have little interest in farming, trade, and crafts—an indifference which matches the standards of a feudal nobility. As they move about with their herds they seem free of ties to soil, job, or any of the mundane economic preoccupations. To the Europeans who ignore the iron necessities of Masai life—grass and water for their herds—this seems like the freedom of a man with a private income.

The Masai, a brave, proud, handsome race are admired by all travelers. Nobody likes the idea of such a people settled, tamed and commercialized.[18]

These fierce six-footers, burnished with grease, are far too proud to work as farm hands and one is forced to draw on inferior stock from the agricultural tribes. . . .
They are aristocratic and are quite conscious of it.[19]

The Masai physical type is also much admired. They tend to be tall, slightly built, with slender hands and feet, aquiline features and thin lips. These traits are found praiseworthy not only for their esthetic appeal but also as the hallmarks of aristocracy. Roderick Cameron praises both Masai beauty and breeding.

Physically, they are extraordinarily beautiful, with slender bones and narrow hips, and the most wonderful rounded muscles and limbs. So delicately built are they that they look more effeminate than the women. But their beauty is entirely masculine. Their breeding shows in their finely-cut nostrils and the precise chiselling of their lips.[20]

The great admiration for the cultural and physical characteristics of the Masai is overshadowed by the esteem given them as outstanding warriors. Historical evidence hardly supports this reputation; as fighters they were not in the same league as the Zulu, the Matabele, the Ashanti, or the Dahomeans. Masai warfare consisted primarily of cattle raiding, which was scarcely full-scale war. The pattern of raid and harassment continued on into the European regimes, causing enough disturbance to require police action by Europeans, but not any serious fighting.[21]

Though raiding was undoubtedly rewarding and perhaps even necessary, this is discounted in the literature. Masai warfare is written of as if it were an end in itself and combat the Masai's only true career. Only by a display of personal valor could manhood be validated, so that when there was no warfare, lion hunting took its place. Their need to protect the cattle from lions is played down, and both warfare and lion hunting are described as expressing the same bravura sportsmanship. Just as British writers overlook economic motives, so they tend to overlook any brutality in Masai raiding. They choose only to see that the Masai fought like gentlemen, gallantly, but without hate or economic necessity. Since the British never had to engage in full-scale warfare against the Masai, and suffered no major losses at their hands, they can afford to see only the elegance and panache of the beautiful young *Moran*, the noble young warrior, playing the game of war. The Masai seem to embody the chivalric ideal of warfare as a sporting contest of brave young men.

The Pax Britannica put an end to Masai forays, but the organization of the youths into warrior groups continued; the *Moran* still paraded in full panoply, and the free life of the pastoralists remained relatively intact. The anthropologist Melville J. Herskovits states that the Masai, like other East African pastoralists, were particularly conservative and resistant to Westernization.[22] The British admire this as proud self-sufficiency. Masai cultural rigidity thus takes on value as part of the fantasy; Cameron sees it as the pride which so befits a noble warrior.

But it is not for their aggressiveness, nor even for their prowess in war, that we admire them today. It is for their beauty, their sense of fair play, and their pride. No Masai will deign to work for a white man. They obstinately refuse to be civilized.[23]

The much-vaunted arrogance of the Masai automatically commands respect, for such supreme confidence in one's own superiority has always been the sign of aristocracy. Many Moslem tribes also elicit Western admiration for the same reasons; they seem unalterably and serenely sure of themselves. The Moslems are not susceptible to European influence, at least to that of the missionaries, and their resistance to Christianity is taken as an index of assurance, integrity, and pride, which is in itself reinforcing evidence of their nobility.

On the surface it seems strange that Islam should be given such prestige by Christian writers. But Islam as a religion and a way of life which elevates warfare, assigns women to the obscurity of purdah, and is altogether male-oriented has had undiminished appeal for the British since the 1850's.

Although himself a stout Christian, Hereward had no wish to attract members of the subject races into the fold, but rather resigned them to the Prophet, whose views on discipline, strong drink and women he considered very sound.[24]

The African literary tradition merges with another important literary tradition about the Bedouins and other pastoral Moslems. Strong interest in the Moslems during the nineteenth and early twentieth centuries is evidenced by the overwhelming success of Burton's Arabian studies and explorations, the works of Charles M. Doughty, T. E. Lawrence, and Gertrude Bell, to say nothing of the novels of Ethel M. Dell. Such writers depicted the Arabs as the romantic and dashing horsemen of the desert. The Moslems of Africa came in, even if only by the back door, for their share of homage on this wave of Arabophilia.

It is consistent with the image of the Land in Amber that the Africans to whom any attention is paid are all admirable. Either they are the unspoiled children of nature dwelling in a primal

Eden, loyal and devoted subjects of empire, or the proud warriors resisting the inroads of Westernization. None of these are tainted by modern civilization, but the most conservative are the most admired. Perhaps this fact explains why Zulu stock is presently lower than it had been in Haggard's day. The Zulu, unlike the Masai, adapted to Western culture; many became Christian; and the warriors were transformed into miners and laborers. None of this is in accord with the nostalgic fantasy of the Land in Amber.

Of all the images this one is the clearest and most consistent reflection of British discontent with modern life. It differs from the Dark Labyrinth in that the dissatisfaction is not based on uncertainty about values. This image expresses great certainty; the writers are very sure that modern civilization is all dross and that true worth is to be found only in the past. The British have created utopian settings in Africa wherein are reconstituted the lost values of earlier times.

CONFRONTATION between the British and Africa is, in the image of the Antagonist, formulated as conflict with a formidable adversary. The metaphor of Africa as a personal antagonist is a staple of the tradition. It is an old figure going back to the explorers' accounts where, Margery Perham and Jack Simmons point out, "the continent plays such an active, and indeed violent part, as to fill something like a distinct role in the drama, certainly that of the villain." [1]

The people of Africa are the merest adjuncts to the central conflict with the continent. At most, the Africans are but the passive objects of British endeavors. As subjects to be governed, ignorant people to be taught, heathens to be converted, patients to be treated, they almost always belong to the faceless, nameless category of "the natives."

The literature since the 1940's has, however, added another dimension to the image of the Antagonist. As the Sleeping Giant, the new aspect complements that of the Antagonist, for it focuses all interest on the Africans. They are the source of Africa's power, and it is their hostility which makes the Giant so threatening a figure.

The older version of the image which relegates the Africans completely to the background, dramatizes the British protagonists more vividly than any other image. So highlighted are the British that any Englishman who can retain his identity and can adhere to his customary code of behavior is acting like a hero. What is merely conventional in England requires courage in Africa, and even the most routine activities, such as serving tea or riding on a train, seem gestures of defiance.

The image of the Antagonist derives from the records of the

early explorers and travelers. The modern literature reinforces it with elaborate accounts of tropical discomforts. Insects, endemic diseases, heat, and loneliness all contribute to the general misery. Unlike their predecessors, the modern Britons appear oversensitive, excessively vulnerable, and prone to interpret every unpleasant experience as an attack upon themselves. Thus, Huxley comments on an African storm that "There's something personal, vindictive, inexorable, about these tropic storms, as if a great mindless beast was out for your blood." [2]

Whatever the irritants are, they are taken as intentional expressions of Africa's hostility. The very first intimation of discomfort confirms the expectation of an all-out attack. This is the self-fulfilling prophecy with which the Englishman makes his own blood run cold. So deeply engrained is this preconception that even where there are no overt manifestations of enmity they are expected, and Africa is seen as "Too careless or too treacherous to threaten . . . with an impassive air that seemed to mask the very claws of danger." [3]

The hostility of the continent is sometimes thought of as defensive, and Africa has consequently erected barriers to ward off intrusion. The hazards, the discomforts, every difficulty the British encounter in Africa are cunningly laid impediments in their path. Van der Post, in the following passage, describes Africa's masterly defense against invasion.

Her coastline, no matter how the sea nibbled at it, kept its defences intact and, when it gave way, retreated in good Macedonian order. To this day the coastline of Africa not only offers no convenient harbours, but most of it, together with the interior, is raised above the water level and the rivers come tumbling out of it in swift, churning, angry torrents that make navigation impossible. Where the earth was not so raised this ancient land threw up vast seas of desert which could be crossed only by a few initiates at their peril. Also, as if to make quite sure that her defences completely sealed Africa off from the outer world, nature developed the most redoubtable champions in the mosquito and tsetse fly and other minute parasites, all able to strike down any invader with a wonderful selection of deadly diseases, from sleeping sickness, malaria, dysentery, and typhoid to leprosy and the bubonic plague. One day I hope to persuade my fellow Africans to put up a monument to the despised mosquito and tsetse fly for discharging so well this task of defending Africa against invasion.[4]

The image depicts the British engaged in perpetual conflict with a powerful enemy. They feel that they can never acclimate to Africa or become inured to its attacks. Eventually all their efforts will be defeated, and Africa, as Greene predicts, will emerge victorious.

. . . they were living here for a short while on the surface of the land, but Africa has the last say, and it said it in the form of rats and ants, of the forest swallowing up the little pits the Dutch prospectors had made and abandoned.[5]

Win, lose, or draw, the conflict with Africa is seen as the crucial test of the true worth of a man's character. The theme of British trial by African ordeal is central in a number of recent novels. In some of them the African experience is the equivalent of ceremonial initiation into manhood. Africa sets the trials which the youth must undergo and the endurance of these vicissitudes makes a man of him. In Hardy's novel, *The Men from the Bush,* two adolescents undergo the ordeal of an African adventure; one is ultimately exposed as a cowardly bully; the other develops into a strong and good man. Even a little boy, the hero of the W. H. Canaway novel, *Find the Boy,* achieves manly strength of character. In *At Fever Pitch* by David Caute the making-of-man theme is painfully literal; a young homosexual, transfigured by his African ordeal, achieves a fully heterosexual experience. Other novels concerned with the testing of character deal rather with the restoration of manhood.[6] The remedial value of African experiences is a popular theme in modern fiction. Ne'er-do-wells, men who have never found themselves, and defeated men all come to Africa— "the cure for the sick heart" [7]—submit to the ordeal, and achieve renascence.

I see a remarkable change in your face. . . . There is something different. I see authority and confidence in your eyes. . . . For every man there comes a testing time that one way or another utterly changes his life. . . . That is a man's critical moment. You will harden, Dennis . . . you will have discovered wonderful new depths in yourself when you finally come through.[8]

In some instances the literature stresses the abrasive effects of Africa that divest a man of his civilized façade, exposing his essential character. In Africa men are "like plucked chickens losing a feather at a time, who would soon find themselves naked before each other with every defect of character plainly visible and beyond disguise."[9] This concept of an abrasion that lays bare all a man's passions and idiosyncrasies is the key to the descriptions of the British settlers in the Kenyan highlands of East Africa. They appear to be singularly eccentric, engaged in a "cult of unconventionality."[10] The Kenyans, Alastair Scobie tells us, "developed a strange 'bush happiness'; let their eccentricities have full rein; and their hair well down."[11]

The suggestion is made that the Highlands, perhaps all the British colonies, are reservoirs of eccentricity, having drained off the deviant members of British society. In this view self-selection partially accounts for the difference between the unconventional colonials and the restrained and orderly society at home. The abrasive effects of Africa only exaggerate pre-existing eccentricities, and it is appropriate in this context to see Africa as the natural refuge for those who are misfits in Britain. Dundas claims that there is "truth in the remark" that the family black sheep can always go to Kenya.[12]

People lacking true strength of character should never have come to Africa. At home they might have lived out their lives securely laced in British conventions, but in Africa they lose their civilized veneer, and with the façade gone nothing remains. The literature recounts numerous tales of men who "went bush," became insane, took to drink, or committed suicide. These cases all demonstrate the consequences of defective character, for, as Hanley sums up, "Africa beat them. It was the kind of place which puts its finger into a man's weakness more swiftly than all the bloody infantry attacks of the war."[13]

Neither the value placed on character nor its definition seem changed since Victorian times. The significant component is still self-discipline. Impulse and spontaneity must be held in constant check, and vigilant social conformity is both means and measure of that control. Confrontation with Africa confirms the value of discipline which alone enables the British to survive intact.

Not all the British engage in open conflict with the Antagonist. The responses of some are defensive, and they attempt to protect themselves by some sort of insulation. Although the insulation takes various forms, all have the express purpose of excluding Africa from their awareness. By means of a precariously maintained nescience they try to negate the presence of the continent.

The oversensitized Englishman resorts to a number of devices to anesthetize himself. The anodynes commonly relied on are made familiar by much usage: drink, flirtations and love affairs, petty intrigue, gossip, and an exaggerated interest in the small change of daily life. The tight little community of beleaguered Englishmen live in a hothouse atmosphere of forced intimacy, depending upon each other for personal relationships, and exploiting each other's personalities for distraction. John R. Wilson's novel, *Double Blind*, conveys the idea that Africa itself enforces such behavior upon the British.

I could imagine the British residents sitting out on their terraces on these soft summer nights, filled with a restlessness that they could not express. It was no wonder they drank too much, that they engaged in listless flirtations with each other's wives. It was almost as if the landscape itself expected it of you.[14]

The pretense that Africa does not exist, seemingly at the root of all the defensive techniques, demands the refuge of a reasonable facsimile of English life. The literature from the mid-nineteenth century on describes the British attempts to re-create small islands of home in "darkest Africa." Up through the imperial period each small replica of Britain was to have been a center for diffusion which would eventually spread light to all the continent. In the twentieth century hope for the spread of civilization has faded, and the British community is only a little clearing in the jungle. By contrast, the surrounding darkness is intensified, while Africa maintains "its habitual vigilance on the frail outposts of the invaders." [15] The only security lies within the British enclave where life goes on much as it would in Britain, and Africa is seldom permitted to intrude. Yet, Hardy writes, it cannot be entirely forgotten.

The room had been painfully English with chintz cushions, a Victorian bureau and a sheaf of mimeographed missionary tracts, a few sepia portraits of solemn cricket teams, curtains out of Manchester cloth. The Lauries had shut the country out. There were no spears or tree-drums or devil-masks on the walls, no carved African figurines, no ebony heads or miniature elephants. "We bake our own bread," Mrs. Laurie said. They could see the panic at the back of her eyes.[16]

The Victorians took for granted their ability to behave as Englishmen wherever they were. It was not considered especially meritorious, but quite simply the natural, inevitable consequence of being English. The modern writers consider that success in carrying on as Englishmen is a triumph of British character. It apparently takes a singularly British form of gallantry to serve tea properly or to grow an English garden in Africa. In the face of Africa, the gesture is made to seem pathetic.

There were drinks, but beyond that there was a tea-table lavishly spread as only the English can spread them. I have sometimes thought since of the Elkington's tea-table round, white, standing with sturdy legs against the green vines of the garden, a thousand miles of Africa receding from its edge.[17]

. . . in Africa, the vision of an English lawn flies over the exiled British imagination like colours nailed to the mast of an out-gunned, sinking ship of the line. The lawns impinged on borders which grew European flowers of a sickly and outraged appearance . . . the African zinnias . . . seemed to be sharing a jibe of their own at the patient, determined nostalgia of the gardens about them.[18]

Whether the British respond directly to the challenge that Africa offers, or retreat from it through evasion and insulation, there seems no doubt that the African experience is preconceived as painful. Against the enmity of Africa the British rely chiefly on the bulwark of British character, either in the personality of the individual or in the maintenance of English forms of behavior. The only defense against the African Antagonist is British character, and the only victory is its vindication.

The complementary image of the Sleeping Giant stresses the antagonism of the people rather than of the continent. It is a new synthesis of conventions in response to the present political situation. The literature has always put emphasis on the vastness of Africa, but this image refers rather to the size of the African population. The older convention of the excessive fertility of the Africans is taken up to become the basis for a new theme. The expanding African population poses the terrifying possibility that the world will be overwhelmed.

As for the people: they pullulate . . . the population will double in 30 years.
The implications are frightening. Adam's instructions were to multiply and replenish the earth, not multiply and despoil it.[19]

The population explosion as a world problem has been sufficiently publicized to make such prognostications seem reasonable to readers. It should be borne in mind, however, that Africa is a far-from-crowded continent. In 1962 the historian, Donald Wiedner, described the demographic facts of Africa as follows:

These more crowded areas (the West-African coast, between the Senegal River and the Cameroons; around the Great Lakes and along the Kenya-Uganda Railway; and in the eastern and southern parts of Southern Rhodesia and the Republic of South Africa) compare roughly to the density variations within France, Ireland or Virginia, but the greater sub-Saharan area has a population about as scattered as that of northern Sweden or the American plains.[20]

The power of the Giant is still unrealized, for Africa has not yet fully awakened. It has only now begun to rouse from its sleep. The conventions that Africa is both ancient and changeless have been revamped, and the many thousand years in which Africa remained unchanging are rephrased as the sleep of the Giant. So the writers speak of "the long trance of African history," [21] "the long sleep of centuries in the sun," [22] "where time made no cross but the present paralleled the eternal," [23] or "a savage land which had sat silent and sick on the edge of history since time began." [24]

Africa had no history, since the passage of time was unmarked by any change. Basil Davidson points out in *The Lost Cities of Africa* that this pervasive concept of an eventless African past even invades the scholarly writing on Africa. His book was written at least partly to counteract the conventional approach which he summarizes as follows: "Nothing with them, as many Europeans thought, could have changed since the age of apes and stone." [25] Elsewhere in the book another passage reads.

The Negro, many have believed, is a man without a past. Black Africa—Africa south of the Sahara desert—is on this view a continent where men by their own efforts have never raised themselves much above the level of the beasts.[26]

This concept of African history stems from the parochial assumption that Europe alone changed throughout the course of time. It is, in fact, a form of solipsism—that Africa had no history because the Europeans played no part in it, and even more were unaware of it.

In place of this relatively unrecorded and little-known history, the writers substitute all the stereotypes of African culture and behavior. Africa existed unchanged, its people in a primal condition and their cultures preserved relics of the first men in the world. The tribes were presumed to have been isolated not only from the events that stirred the rest of mankind but also from each other. Tribal life was self-contained and savage, the people aware of outsiders only as predators or victims. Tribesmen were motivated purely by tribal traditions or by instinct.

The stasis of Africa was ended only by the coming of the Europeans. The arrival of civilized men provided the stimulus for its emergence from the archaic past. The writing assumes that without this contact Africa would yet be within the changeless cycle of Stone Age life. Cloete illustrates with what reluctance Africa presumably responded to the prod of European entry.

The African giant . . . was throwing off his chains. He was flexing his muscles. . . . And the rest of African habit and custom had been disturbed, the pattern of 10,000 years shattered in this period of transition. The giant [was] fevered by a dream . . . he wanted to go back into the security of the ancient tribal womb where everything was unchanging and changeless.[27]

So long as the Giant remained inviolate and undisturbed he presented no threat, but the attempt to bring the benefits of civilization to Africa roused it from its centuries-long lethargy. Whatever uneasiness or discomfort the Europeans must endure in this changing Africa are, therefore, to be laid at their own doorstep. Europe alone bears the responsibility for what ensues. Huxley states that ". . . we must answer for our own Frankensteins." [28] And Julian Mockford uses exactly the same idiom.

Its millions are stirring like a giant—perhaps, from the White man's point of view, like a Frankenstein largely of his own creation; a Frankenstein *ex machina*, from the *Pax Britannica* no less.[29]

Obviously the British mission to bring enlightenment has gone wrong somewhere. If all the effort, the pouring into Africa of wealth and lives, has resulted in a Frankenstein monster then the British have failed signally. The gulf was too deep and wide, the crossing unsuccessful, the bridge too fragile, and the transfer of values and goods incomplete. All they feel they have done was to goad Africa from somnolence and to set a resentful Giant in motion. Van der Post indicates that thus were created the conditions for chaos.

. . . somewhere in Africa's hidden being is piling up a sinister power of accumulated energy sufficient to shatter the world that is taking away its soul. Africa is being charged like one of the electronic piles used to split the atom. For Africa, from earth and beast, up to the most intelligent of its indigenous children is not letting this loss of soul take place without a terrible struggle. Even the soil of Africa, this ancient red soil, founded on the original rock of the earth, is rebelling against European methods. . . .[30]

The stirring up of the Giant to threaten the entire world is an elaborate hyperbole that, literally speaking, comes down to African resistance to colonialism. After the end of World War II movements toward African independence accelerated. Nationalism is the new dynamic factor in African politics, and in the literature nationalism is generally equated with antiwhite attitudes. This is a situation scarcely calculated to maintain British equanimity in their relations with their former colonies.

No armed might, no amount of British courage can restore their former position in Africa. The British hark back to past glories, good works, and individual sacrifice as they deplore the course of events. Quite often they blame their own leniency toward the Africans for what has occurred. By allowing the Africans too much freedom, they feel they have undermined their own strength. The response to their present weakness is resentful, frightened, and nostalgic for a past effectiveness.

In the literature from the 1930's on, the British seem profoundly pessimistic about their future in Africa. Their expulsion was inevitable, their accomplishments negated, their works destroyed, and they will be uncompensated by any gratitude or even acknowledgment of the debt they feel Africa owes them.

I thought we came out here to serve these black primitives; we bring them science, the light of progress—and for what? One could write their expressions of gratitude on the head of a pin. . . .
    When they throw us out of Africa they won't even lift a hand to wave us goodbye.[31]

The British are even more pessimistic concerning the welfare of independent Africa. Sir Charles Dundas, although more sanguine than most, questions the ability of Africa to succeed on its own: "Whether the African by himself can master both the old and new spirit of his race remains to be seen." [32] The majority of writers are certain that Africa cannot succeed without European guidance and control. Cary, for example, feels that independent Africa is bound to fail.

My book was meant to show certain men and their problems in the tragic background of a continent still little advanced from the Stone Age, and therefore exposed, like no other, to the impact of modern turmoil. An overcrowded raft manned by children who had never seen the sea would have a better chance in a typhoon.[33]

This despondent outlook is based upon the familiar premise that the Africans are unable to grasp the essentials of civilization. Only partially acculturated, half-educated and half-Christianized, they are not yet ready to guide their own destiny. The influence of the West prematurely sparked African nationalism and independence. The desire of the Africans for self-government far outran their acceptance or even understanding of the responsibilities of freedom. None of the Africans, say the writers, can adequately replace European colonial officials. Old-style African chiefs are certainly not competent to govern modern states. Leaders must be recruited from the acculturated group whose very Westernization makes them mistrusted. The traditional image of the Westernized African is transferred to the new elite. They are described as ruthless, exploitive, and tyrannical, and they will only restore the older patterns of African despotism, or, perhaps even worse, open the way to complete anarchy.

I've had enough. Been working over fifteen years with these black bastards and never met a straight one yet and I've been all over the country too. What I say is—hand the bloody place over to them— let them run it . . . and stand back and watch the fireworks. Look at the balls up in Ghana. Bribery and corruption, fighting and murder, the prisons full of the opposition. . . .[34]

Even if the new leaders were to prove politically effective it would be small comfort to the British who see their primary motivation as antiwhite. Effective leadership is thus as much to be feared as ineffective rule. Ineptitude will result in a chaotic eruption of Africa's power, but effectiveness will be equally devastating because of its hostile intent.

The writers, who see the new Africa as a continent where brutish and ignorant masses are ruled by a corrupt and despotic leadership, predict that the new Africa will be in many ways much like the old Africa. There is bound to be a reversion to savagery; all the horrors of a savage condition will sweep away whatever amelioration had been achieved. Lady Joy Packer writes of the colonial period that ". . . this era of African prosperity and education . . . was but a flash between the dark and the dark." [35]

Literary disquietude about African reversion to savagery is all the greater since the reversion is never simply envisioned as the Giant's return to sleep. Africa is awake and moving and will remain a threat to civilization and its values. In *Red Rock Wilderness* Huxley sees the political changes on the continent as

. . . a battle for the continent, and perhaps even more than that, for the survival of the West. It is a battle between the forces of reason, progress and civilization and the forces of fear, hatred and tyranny— the forces of darkness.[36]

The old conventions and stereotypes have all been resynthesized in the image of the Giant to express the British sense of failure at colonialism and the mission to civilize. The failure is rationalized by the restatement of the impossibility of bridging the Abysmal Gulf which eternally separates Africa from the West. At best, whatever the Africans have adopted of civilization provides them with a thin veneer, false values, and perhaps new motivations and mechanisms for the expression of old savagery. Whatever rationalizations are made, the sense of failure lies just below the surface. The good intentions and the hard work of empire have gone for nought. Enlightenment wakened the Giant, and awake, he exerted his enormous power to reject the givers and their gifts. They earned for their pains not gratitude or acceptance but hate and angry rejection. Even the glib rationales do not quite conceal a hurt bewilderment.

The predominant response to the British sense of failure and to

African rejection is one of reciprocal hostility. Most of the images of the continent presume Africa to be hostile to the British, but heretofore, the British recorded little outright hostility in themselves. At worst, the British response to Africa was ambivalent. At its best it was clearly a case of true love. Africa may have been hostile to the British, but they were entranced with Africa. Reciprocation of the hostility is a newer component; the projection has come full circle.

The entire image is, in fact, a totally hostile one. In the other images hostility is covert, palliated, and perhaps even masked by depictions of devoted servants, loyal subjects, cooperative chiefs, and even noble savages. The British laid claim to love from at least some of the Africans, a love that was sometimes as specious as was perhaps the claim to it. Specious or not, this love of the Africans for their British masters persists in the literature and is a significant expression of British faith in their own goodness and good will. The image of the Sleeping Giant contains no such mitigating good will or expectation of love.

The literature attributes British failure to civilize to the inherent savagery of the Africans, but along with this explanation a certain discomfiture is frequently expressed. The writers fear that African rejection of British values may be justifiable. Their *post hoc* reasoning is that they may have been rejected by Africa because what they were doing in Africa was not worth doing. They, themselves, are no longer certain. In the final analysis, all they have done is to substitute new problems as perplexing and insoluble as the old. In an attempt to assess the final value of British rule in Africa, Dorothy Wellesley questions the worth of Western civilization altogether.

Personally I have never been able to decide whether or not Western civilization is desirable even in Europe. . . . This is one of the questions which many of us, perhaps, will never be quite sure about. . . . The worst perhaps that can be said of Imperialism is that it gives to the native a new set of troubles in exchange for the old.[37]

The major difference between twentieth- and nineteenth-century writing on Africa is in the self-image of the British. The confidence of the empire-builders is lost in the twentieth century. The literary tradition, however, perpetuates the older stereotypes and, indeed, demonstrates their continued vitality. The liquidation of the empire by no means bankrupted the traditional images. On the contrary, the new situation has been as much a stimulus for proliferation of the tradition as had been the growth of empire.

chapter ten
the british self-image

THROUGHOUT the literature the image of Africa and the British image of themselves are intimately related; one is the obverse of the other. Africa *is* whatever the British *are not*. The delineation of Africa by means of a set of contrasts is, therefore, dependent upon the British view of themselves. This self-image is not limited to the literature on Africa, but does conform to other evaluations of the British and genuinely seems to express British values and attitudes.

Seen through British eyes, Britain and Africa represent the two poles of a single system of values. These are variously phrased as light opposed to darkness, civilization to savagery, good to evil. Africa is the "continent of dark negation." Contrast with it demonstrates the nature of these values, and confrontation confirms their worth.

The literature on Africa from both the Victorian and the modern periods expresses the same ideals of character, among which discipline and courage are the most important. A man should be so disciplined that he never loses self-control, and his behavior conforms to a rigorous code no matter what the situation. The capacity for heroism, whether in sport or warfare, is the essence of character.

Both Victorian and modern writers share the belief that such character is particularly manifested by members of the upper classes. The literary tradition stresses that the British in Africa are gentlemen. Until well into the nineteenth century the British in Africa were often admittedly from less elevated ranks of society. Class consciousness became a vital aspect of the British self-image only in the mid-nineteenth century and permeated all the subsequent literature.

The modern literature does, however, differ from the Victorian by lessened confidence in England. The exercise of discipline and the display of courage seem underrated and unrewarded. Owing to the changed social structure, England is no longer governed by gentlemen. They have, thus, lost their chief role, and their values are anachronistic. The worth of these values remains an article of faith, but modern England has gone astray. Progress has not fulfilled the promise it held for the Victorians. England is no longer what it was—the nation which created and was created by men of character.

It is an oft-repeated comment in the African literature that only gentlemen should be in positions of authority, since they alone have the requisite character. Whether as army officer, civil servant, or private citizen, an English gentleman, no matter what his feelings, must always be in sufficient command of himself to command others, and to do so justly and effectively. The literature indicates that in the service of the empire discipline demonstrated its worth. In this respect the literature on Africa is no different from the literature on other parts of the British Empire. In Africa, India or anywhere else it is the English gentleman who keeps the imperial sun from setting.

The most effective agency for making gentlemen out of boys is generally thought to be the English public school. There is inculcated the assurance of superior status and the character worthy of its privileges. It is also in the public schools that boys are trained to leadership. Hilaire Belloc terms the public schools "seminaries for the English governing class," [1] and James Wellard gives ironic consent to this definition.

The major reward of attending a public school is the firm assurance which never leaves the alumnus afterward, that . . . they are the cream of society and all the rest, the skimmed milk. . . . This simple and useful classification of humanity into two parts is indispensable in later life, in the executive and administrative posts for which public school boys are destined. Hence, in their dealings with subordinates and foreigners and all lesser breeds without the law, these model Englishmen . . . have the unshakeable conviction of intrinsic superiority. Obviously such a conviction together with a complete imperviousness to ideas makes them inviolate and invincible.[2]

The public school builds character, and character is the essential quality of a gentleman. It is precisely because of his character that a gentleman can be entrusted with the welfare of his country. Philip Carr and J. D. Scott, among many other commentators on English life, indicate that in the scale of British values character far outweighs expertise.

What is certain is that the public schools produce a type of character which has been of great service to the state, as well as being admirable in itself. The system encourages the sense of responsibility; but it tames arrogance and induces modesty. It brings the capacity for practical judgement to early maturity; but it also develops the sense of fairness in general and justice to inferiors in particular.[3]

. . . the belief that the best kind of man to run anything important, from a merchant banking firm to an African colony or the British embassy in Moscow, is a one-time Captain of the Eton cricket eleven with a good second-class University degree in Classics. . . . It is a source of bitterness to many people that so many important posts are now going to experts, clever men specially trained, who because of their special training cannot take a broad view and because of their cleverness are probably dishonourable and possibly cowardly.[4]

Some writers are approving, others are hostile, and still others are ironic about the character fostered by the public schools. Yet there is consensus that a code of behavior is strongly inculcated and that the code requires a self-abnegating devotion to one's obligations. A gentleman is not governed by emotions or by considerations of his own advantage but by the firmly implanted standards of his class. George Orwell notes the effectiveness of that training.

After all, they belonged to a class with a certain tradition, they had been to public schools where the duty of dying for your country, if necessary, is laid down as the first and greatest of the commandments. They had to *feel* themselves true patriots. . . .[5]

The mainspring of the gentleman's character is self-control, for only the unrelenting inhibition of impulse permits him to abide by a code that requires conformity in all things, from the style of dress to the manner of death. The goal of public-school education is thus not the full development of the individual, but the conquest of self. Martin Green considers such an education to be appallingly effective.

. . . a quality . . . lies deep in most modern British figures of authority and intelligence . . . a quality of a revenge taken on one's own spontaneity . . . the source of their energy is a cold joy in the defeat of humanity in themselves and in others.[6]

The literature on the British at home and the African literature both highlight their discussions of the value of discipline by the use of contrast, in one instance with the Africans, and in the other with the lower classes. As Harold Nicolson so coolly phrases it, "internal and external proletariats" are equivalents,[7] and assignment to the category of lesser breed can, obviously, be made either on the basis of race or class. Lower classes, like Africans, lack self-control. For those writers who are critical of the social order, the lack has positive value, and they credit the lower classes with greater warmth, spontaneity, and humanity.[8] This, too, has its parallel in the literature on Africa where writers who question the value system express admiration or envy of the emotional freedom of the Africans.

The writers in both samples, no matter what their point of view, seem to belong to the upper classes. This seems particularly characteristic of the writers on Africa. The generalization is, of course, more nearly valid if one defines upper class quite broadly. Apparently a not-too-rigid definition is permissible. Authorities such as G. D. H. Cole, David C. Marsh, and T. H. Pear suggest that the upper class shades into the upper middle class of intelligentsia, higher civil servants, professional men, and so on.[9] The real break in the English class structure is thus somewhere within the middle class. The significant distinction is between those who have had a public-school education and those who have not. By this token most English writers belong, as Martin Green states, to the upper classes.

There have never been any working-class writers in England. And during this century, of course, literature has retreated up the social ladder. All our authors are public schoolboys—Waugh, Greene, Auden, Isherwood, Connolly, even Orwell. . . . [Lawrence as the chief exception]. They are "British" gentlemen, ruling class.[10]

Our information on the values of the upper classes, therefore, derives from descriptions given by their members. While these writers have the advantage of intimate knowledge, their observations and judgments are bound to be subjective. Despite their similar social status, the writers differ markedly from one another and have varied political points of view. Nevertheless, the descriptions are all quite consistent, whether the writer is as aloof as Denis W. Brogan, as scornful as Green and Orwell, or as approving as Carr and Nicolson. Consensus among such different writers can hopefully be taken as an indication of reliability, for these literary, impressionistic materials are the only data available. As Pear so justly points out, "there has been little field-work among the English upper class." [11]

Objective studies of the lower classes have, however, been conducted by social scientists. For the most part field work among the English is of the kind Geoffrey Gorer terms " 'slumming sociology,' descriptions of how 'the other half' lives and works." [12] Even in B. M. Spinley's comparative study of upper- and lower-class patterns, the "Deprived" are much more fully described than the "Privileged." [13] Although the studies of the lowest levels of British society are objective and scholarly, they tend to be contrastive in their point of view and so bear a certain resemblance to the literary accounts of the Africans. They, too, "emphasize the differences, not the similarities, between the people studied and the people likely to read the studies." [14] For this reason Gorer's book, *Exploring English Character*, has special value. Although the social extremes are underrepresented, this study includes the large middle segment of English society, which has hitherto been quite neglected. It is worth noticing that despite considerable criticism of the Gorer study, there is as much confirmation of his findings. Since Gorer, furthermore, addresses himself specifically to the nature of English values and attitudes, his work is particularly pertinent.

The most striking conclusion that can be drawn from the studies made by Gorer and others is that the values of the lower middle class and upper working class in English society are similar to those of the upper class. Most writers on English society greatly exaggerate the difference in values between their own class and the rest of English society. The leveling processes of the present century, at least, seem to have created a more homogeneous society than is generally acknowledged. This may, in part, explain the extreme importance attached to speech habits; as other differences become less apparent the public-school or upper-class dialect serves as the most significant, overt symbol of social distinction.

For the English, self-control is both a value in itself and the basis for the entire complex of virtues labeled "character." Implicit in the value of self-control is the underlying puritanical assumption that human beings are naturally evil. Since spontaneous behavior is aggressive and destructive, self-conquest not self-realization is the desired end in the rearing of children. Parents and their surrogates must impose a severe discipline upon children in order to bring all the natural, antisocial tendencies of the self under control.

The formation of a good English character depends on the parents imposing suitable disciplines as early as possible; the child's character will be spoiled if the discipline is insufficient or not applied soon enough . . . discipline, habit training, is good in itself, and valuable for the formation of a good character, almost without regard to the habits trained or imposed.[15]

Adults who cannot or do not discipline themselves must be controlled by those who do. The demand that authorities take a firm stand, the approbation of what has been till recently a very harsh penal code, seem to derive from this attitude. And without question it is reflected in the African material. The use of force against their African subjects was justified by the English in the name of discipline, and as with children, the Africans were punished for their own good.

To Gorer as well as to other commentators the control of aggression seems the "central problem for the understanding of the English character." [16] Gorer accounts for the repression of other emotions and impulses as by-products, since "the habits of rigid self-control, which we have postulated in the case of aggression, would be likely to generalize to all forms of self-expression." [17] Whether or not control of aggression plays the dynamic, causative role Gorer assigns to it, the fact remains that aggression is firmly controlled. Scott, in his comments on Gorer, writes that he is "quite ready to accept the proposition that every Englishman is his own policeman," [18] and that self-discipline is the chief cause of the orderliness and absence of violence in English society.

Gorer believes that the psychic energy involved in aggression and its control "is not entirely dissipated; it finds outlets in a number of different ways, many of them symbolic." [19] He notes the possibilities in gardening, mastery over pets, and the severe disciplining of children as permitted outlets for aggression. (Perhaps the vicarious excitement to be found in the reading of the literature on Africa is one of them.) And warfare, of course, provides or once did provide an entirely legitimate expression of aggression. In war anger may be fully released because it is in a good cause, and not the indulgence of base instincts.

Sport, particularly the hunting of big game, is an obvious and highly valued outlet for aggression. The delight in hunting and the attraction to Africa because it provides good sport is one of the mainstays of the literature on Africa. But there is more to the satisfaction found in hunting than release of aggression. Sport has its own code: Carr pronounces the judgment that "A true sportsman will refuse to take the opportunity of achieving an easy success." [20] The enormous satisfaction in enduring hardship and discomfort that has always been so much part of the self-image of the British in Africa is related to the rejection of "easy success." Physical discomfort takes on a moral quality, for suffering endured is proof of self-mastery. Neither self-pity nor self-indulgence have deflected the Englishman from his goal. Even more vital is the element of risk; the sportsman faces danger in his pursuit of game and thereby gains assurance that he has overcome fear. Carr defines the best sport as "Difficulty, fatigue, hardship, danger—these are what make the greatest sport; and such magnets are they that men will deliberately seek them. . . ." [21]

The whole lure of Africa is implicitly predicated in Carr's exposition of the sporting spirit: "that a thing may be worth doing for the sake of the adventure—that is, for the sake of the very danger and the discomfort." [22] In Africa, where hardship and danger were embraced with self-congratulatory zeal, these multiple values of release of aggression and the demonstration of control over fear and self-indulgence can be fully realized.

The ethical import of sportsmanship and the code of fair play are extended into all aspects of life. If life can be thought of as a game, then profound emotion is uncalled for, and the English distrust of emotion and its repression are justified. Whether in sport, war, or all of life, there is, therefore, every need for good form and very little need for strong feeling.

The sporting spirit even means that one must never forget that the whole of life is only a game, which must be played keenly, according to the rules, but without taking the whole thing too seriously, and that its greatest moments should be lived not only with a sense of the game, but with a sense of the sports of the field. [23]

The ethos in which games serve as a model for life has extended the premium on team spirit to a general male solidarity. The segregation of the sexes begins in the schools and tends to persist throughout life. This becomes especially noticeable in leisure pursuits. Carr, for example, attributes the prevalence of men's clubs, mainly an upper-class habit, to a "profound social instinct of the Englishman, the separation of the sexes for relaxation." [24] This "instinct" seems characteristic of all classes, however, including slum dwellers and coal miners as described by Norman Dennis, Fernando Henriques, and Clifford Slaughter.

Men grow into a status, together with their age-mates, which makes them eligible for participation in these institutions and activities. At the same time they grow into a set of attitudes and ideas which very consciously exclude women from the activities and permitted liberties of the male group, which can be said to constitute a type of secret society.[25]

These attitudes are also reflected in the African literature where the African experience symbolizes the entrance of the Englishman into an exclusive and esoteric male society. Africa itself provides the ordeal which initiates the youth into the society of men. It is a secret society given no overt formal expression, but the members know one another. They recognize their fellows even over the barriers of race and culture. The Masai and the Zulu are described as such true men, blood brothers to the English—brave, disciplined, and indifferent to women.

The exclusiveness of male society is inevitably accompanied by a sense of masculine superiority to which women give assent. Gorer reports that women would like to join in men's associations and activities if they were permitted.[26] It is interesting to notice how often the African literature tells of British ladies who avail themselves of the unusual opportunities in Africa to behave like gentlemen and sportsmen.

The generally masculine tone of the English ethos tends to devalue women and to set them apart. Some authorities believe that sex, as a social category, leads to greater differences in attitudes and values than any other form of social differentiation.[27] Although legally women have equal status with men, it would appear that women, by and large, are social inferiors who have only limited significance in the lives of men.

From boyhood into manhood the small groups in which males share their actions and thoughts maintain and strengthen the ideas of manliness being opposed to anything to do with girls and women, except in terms of sexual conquest . . . and is invariably reasserted completely after the early years of marriage.[28]

The sociological study of an English coal-mining town from which the above was taken also contains a statement of an attitude toward women that matches the British image of African women.

"In such an ideology women can only be objects of lust, mothers and domestic servants." [29] And the role of an English mother has been described by James H. Wellard as one of "loving drudgery." [30] African and English women are perceived in much the same terms.

Studies which attempt some comparison between English and American sexual behavior concur in their findings that the English, both men and women, are considerably less active sexually than the Americans.[31] The rather general attitude reported by Slater and Woodside in their study of British marriage, that "sex is a duty and women are not trained to expect any particular pleasure," [32] can account for the English woman's indifference. Although sex is deemed a masculine prerogative, men also tend to minimize its importance. Sexual attraction is not considered a reason for marriage or a valuable attribute of one's wife. In fact, a lack of interest in sex on the part of both husband and wife is a matter for complacent, mutual congratulation. Strong sexual feelings suffer the same repression to which all emotion is subject. Scott rather sadly remarks that "British men are not generally *en rapport* with women; it has been questioned whether they are profoundly *en rapport* with pleasure." [33]

There are indications, however, that these attitudes of devaluation of women and of sexuality are presently undergoing some change. The relationship between spouses, it is felt, ought to be more of a partnership than has been customary. In the newer suburbs husband and wife share a common interest in their home, and more of the man's leisure time is spent there with his wife than at a pub with other men. More demands are made on marriage for greater compatibility, emotional responsiveness and sexual satisfaction. If some recent British films and novels are to be taken at face value, the change is a very marked one, especially among the young. It is interesting, however, that the bold depiction of sexuality in the films is not accompanied by any elevation of the status of women, but merely a greater emphasis upon them as sex-objects. These attitudes are echoed in the newer image of Africa, which surrounds the continent with an aura of sexuality and grants African women an intense if passive sexuality.

It is not only in marriage that the English look for greater gratifications. Since World War II, the English standard of living has gone up. Higher wages and the Welfare State have made possible increased consumption. Whatever moral value discomfort may have had for gentlemen, it has not inhibited the working-class Englishman, the chief beneficiary of the postwar situation, from availing himself of the opportunities to enjoy better housing, clothing, and other comforts.

Except for such limited change, the English value system seems intact. Most of Gorer's list of constants—"love of freedom; fortitude; a low interest in sexual activity . . . a strong belief in the value of education for the formation of character; consideration . . . for the feelings of other people" [34]—are values still firmly held by most Englishmen. Yet there is still the feeling that gentlemen and their values have no place in modern England, and it pervades the literature on Africa and on England.

For the Welfare State is no gentleman's country, and an educated Englishman, whatever he may think about it cannot feel it to be anything but unpalatable, or at best unexciting. . . . The facts of life in England in the twentieth century . . . either distress or bore every man of sensibility and discrimination in the country. And yet more people have better health, more money, better education, etc., etc., than ever before. But it is no longer a gentleman's country, and all men of sensibility are gentlemen. [35]

The distress Green attributes to men of "sensibility and discrimination" can hardly be accounted for on the grounds of pure selfishness. Gentlemen surely do not so bitterly begrudge their countrymen access to better health, education, and more comfort. But improvement in the circumstances of the lower classes has been accompanied by a sense of insecurity of tenure in the upper classes. Studies by David Glass and his associates indicate a fairly high rate of downward mobility in recent times.[36] Although G. D. H. Cole partly questions the validity of these findings,[37] they would seem to indicate some realistic basis for the disquietude of the upper classes.

The power position of the upper classes appears weakened. The products of the public schools no longer feel assured of monopoly of leadership in the civil service or the professions. The state-supported schools are modeled on the public schools, and although they cannot give the cachet of superior social status, they do provide an adequate education. They enable their students to qualify for a variety of positions in the modern world where "examination is exalted above personality and trial of personal worth." [38] Even army commissions are no longer prerogatives of the upper classes, for in modern warfare technical skills seem more important than character. Pear suggests that "character" might even be a handicap, since "So far as the Army is concerned, atom- and germ-warfare and the use of hydrogen bombs will never be activities suitable for gentlemen—or sportsmen. . . ." [39]

The sense of alienation reported by upper-class writers is only partly based on the threat, and it is as yet only a threat, to their status. Their values cannot be merely equated with the retention of privilege; a code that places so much more value on discipline than on gratification is probably too austere to permit this. The English do believe that the self-disciplined life is the good life and, therefore, self-rewarding, that " 'righteousness' does in fact exalt a nation." [40] But it is just this sense of exaltation that is now missing. The ideological foundations that gave meaning to self-discipline have been weakened, whether they were found in religion, progress, or imperialism.

Orwell links the decline of the empire with a more profound weakening of British morale.[41] Sir John Strachey, who takes even more pride in the dissolution of the empire than he does in its acquisition, writes of the need for some new great enterprise to reinvigorate English morale.

It will not do us much good to exhibit all the wisdom and moderation in the world, if we do not find some fresh national purpose, capable of inspiring the spirit and energies of the British people. For to a considerable extent the enlargement or maintenance of the empire has been our national purpose. . . . Yet we shall stagnate unless we can find other purposes to satisfy our hearts.[42]

Responsibility for the empire may well have given purpose and meaning to the austere, self-depriving character of the English.

Imperial England was powerful and wealthy, and as Brogan says, "Virtue was its own reward, and who, looking at the reward, could doubt the virtue?" [43] It is, however, open to question whether imperialism was a truly national ideology. It was more closely allied to the interests of the upper classes, and it was they, rather than the lower classes, who suffered the greater moral loss. David Frost and Anthony Jay do point out that the British of all classes have been deprived by loss of opportunities for validation of manhood.

> Where do you find the challenge, the excitement, the stretching of your capabilities, the test of your courage and nerve that some people need to make them feel that they are living and not just existing. . . . There was a time when you could enlist as a soldier and fight wars; but not any more. There was a time when you could go out to a colony, open up the West, pioneer new frontiers; but not any more.[44]

Protestant Christianity was a system of belief which certainly affected all the social levels of England, and according to the historian K. B. Smellie, ". . . the protestant ethic . . . provided . . . the metaphysical basis for the decencies we still in general observe." [45] Gorer also holds religion to be the strongest sanction for the English moral code.[46] Other accounts, however, stress the weakening of religious faith both in regard to church attendance and to any genuine concern with religion. This loss of faith is regretted because morality is thereby weakened and because human beings have need for faith.[47]

None of the nineteenth-century articles of faith seem secure in the twentieth century. Along with imperialism and religion, the belief in science and progress has been shaken. The cause of progress may once have provided the higher purpose that justified self-denial, but the modern Englishman cannot be confident that social change, increase in scientific knowledge, and expansion of industry will result in the improvement of mankind. Progress has lost its role as a validating purpose, and even more, the direction "progress" has taken seems antithetical to the older values. Orwell is, somewhat unexpectedly, one of the harshest critics of "progress." For his opinion is that "The tendency of mechanical progress is to make your environment safe and soft; and yet you are striving to keep yourself brave and hard." [48] In a world made "safe for little fat men" [49] strength of character and will are superfluous.

Every attitude, major or minor, to be found projected in the literature on Africa has its counterpart expressly stated in the commentaries on England, with one exception—racism. Yet racism is one of the fundamental components of the British literary tradition about Africa; it is equally prevalent in the writing on India, or for that matter, wherever non-white populations come under discussion. Its almost complete omission in the British self-commentary is, therefore, the more striking. Some mention is made of xenophobia, more often phrased as insularity, but even then, it is dismissed as a minor idiosyncrasy, or an attitude held by the ill-educated. Recent events in Great Britain, however, force the recognition that racism is endemic in the whole society. That the British analysts of their own culture do not discuss it indicates a peculiar sort of nescience.

Speculation on this lack of awareness suggests several possible causes. It may be that the liberal and humanitarian values of the British interdict recognition of so antithetical a concept as racism. It is also true that until recently the issue did not have to be faced at home. Racism could be projected out onto the darker-skinned populations of the colonies and there phrased in terms of the master-subject relationship. There had been relatively few non-whites in England, and they were mostly transient students and visitors to whom the British were kind and hospitable, even if patronizing. But the recent immigrants from the former colonies are not transients, nor are they subjects; they are peers to be accorded equal treatment. Great Britain has become a multiracial society in which the new relationship of black and white has evoked the open expression of British racism in acts of discrimination, immigration laws, and race riots.

Contemporary England seems to have undergone a moral revolution evidenced by frivolity in fashions, overt sexuality, youthful rebellion, and aggressive behavior. But one may question whether this self-indulgence is a manifestation of a new hedonism or the froth churned up by the search for new moral purpose. Frost and Jay suggest that the British take up again their mission to civilize, this time donning the mantle of Athens to bring culture and refinement to the new Romans across the Atlantic.[50] Certainly the "angry young men" seem as profoundly motivated by the Protestant passion for righteousness as their Victorian forebears were. They hold the values of the past firmly enough to use them as standards by which to judge and condemn the present.

The values of character have changed less than other aspects of British culture. Victorian values are retained in British writing about themselves and about Africa. And it is the British concept of themselves which has determined their concept of Africa.

Four centuries of writing about Africa have produced a literature which describes not Africa but the British response to it. The literature persistently recounts the fantasy of the Englishman in confrontation with Africa. As in a morality play, the British and the Africans are the exemplars of civilization and savagery, respectively. In the Victorian version civilization equalled the positive good and savagery its abhorrent negation. Modern writers often reverse the equation as an expression of their uncertainties. Whether confident or doubtful, the writers describe Africa in the same conventions. The image of Africa remains the negative reflection, the shadow, of the British self-image.

notes

Preface

1. Joyce Cary, *The Case for African Freedom* (London, 1944), p. 135.
2. Joyce Cary, *The African Witch* (London, 1951), p. 88.
3. Elspeth Huxley, *Four Guineas* (London, 1954), p. 205.
4. Tom Stacey, *The Brothers M* (New York, 1961), p. 158.

Introduction

1. Katherine George, "The Civilized West Looks at Primitive Africa: 1400–1800," *Isis,* 49 (1958), pp. 62–72.

Chapter I
Commerce in Commodities and Human Beings

1. Richard Hakluyt, *Voyages,* Vol. IV (Glasgow, 1904), p. 194.
2. *Ibid.,* VI, 180.
3. Hakluyt, IV, VI, XI (1904 ed.); Samuel Purchas, *Purchas, His Pilgrimes* (Glasgow, 1905), VI.
4. Richard Jobson, *The Golden Trade, or a Discovery of the River Gambia* (London, 1623).
5. Hakluyt, VI, 167–72.
6. Eden, in J. W. Blake, *Europeans in West Africa,* Vol. II (London, 1942), p. 289.
7. Hakluyt, VI, 184–85.
8. *Ibid.,* p. 151.
9. Towerson, in J. W. Blake, *Europeans in West Africa,* p. 292.
10. Hakluyt, VI, 321.
11. J. Churchill, *Collections of Voyages and Travels* (London, Vols., I–IV, 1704; V–VI, 1752).
12. Archibald Dalzel, *The History of Dahomy, an inland kingdom of Africa* (London, 1793); Robert Norris, *Memories of the Reign of Bosse Whadee, King of Dahomey* (London, 1789); William Snelgrave,

A *New Account of Some Parts of Guinea and the Slave Trade* (London, 1734); William Smith, *New Voyage to Guinea* (London, 1744).

13. Phillips, in Churchill, *Collection*, VI, 147.

14. Dalzel, *Dahomy*, p. vii.

15. Norris, *Memories*, p. 157.

16. Dalzel, *Dahomy*, pp. xxiv–xxv.

17. Basil Davidson, *Black Mother* (Boston, 1961), p. xvii.

18. Michel Adanson, in Wylie Sypher, *Guinea's Captive Kings: British Anti-Slavery Literature of the XVIII Century* (Chapel Hill, 1941), p. 57.

19. Robert Burns, in E. B. Dykes, *The Negro in English Romantic Thought* (Washington, 1942), p. 20.

20. Mrs. Aphra Behn, *Oroonoko* (London, c. 1677).

21. *Ibid.*, p. 23.

22. Reverend William Dodd, *The Epistle of Zara at the Court of Anamboe, to the African Prince Now in England,* in Dodsley's *Collections* (London, 1783), IV, 222.

23. Roy Harvey Pearce, *The Savages of America* (Baltimore, 1953).

The Early Nineteenth Century: West Africa

1. Plan of the Association from the *Proceedings of the Association for Promoting the Discovery of the Interior Parts of Africa* (London, 1790).

2. Hugh Clapperton, *Journal of a Second Expedition into the Interior of Africa, and the Journal of Richard Lander* (Philadelphia, 1829), p. 3.

3. Captain William Allen and T. R. H. Thompson, *Narrative of the Expedition to the River Niger in 1841,* 2 vols. (London, 1848), I, 218–19.

4. Thomas Thompson, 1758; John Beecham, 1841; T. B. Freeman, 1844; Samuel Crowther, 1855.

5. Reverend R. Montgomery, "Proceedings of the First Public Meeting of the Glasgow Society" in L. J. Saunders, *Scottish Democracy, 1815–1840: The Social and Intellectual Background* (London and Edinburgh, 1950), p. 393.

6. Alexander Laing, *Travels in the Timannee, Kooranko and Soolima Countries* (London, 1825), p. 320.

7. Wallace Notestein, *The Scot in History* (New Haven, 1949), pp. 96, 187.

8. Mungo Park was a physician, Hugh Clapperton an officer in the Navy, and Alexander Laing in the Army; John Duncan had been in the Life Guards. Richard Lander was a literate "Gentleman's gentle-

man." William Baikie was a surgeon and had achieved distinction as a naturalist. At the times of Thomas Bowdich's mission to Ashanti he was a "writer" (clerk) with the African Company of Merchants and later (1820) he lived in Paris, writing and studying mathematics and natural science.

9. Mungo Park, *Travels in the Interior Districts of Africa, 1795, 1796 and 1797* (London, 1799), pp. 62–63.

10. Richard and John Lander, *Journal of an Expedition to Explore the Course and Termination of the Niger*, 2 vols. (New York, 1833), II, 154; see also pp. 62 and 63.

11. Mungo Park, *Journal of a Mission to the Interior of Africa in the year 1805* (Philadelphia, 1815), p. 163.

12. Park, *Travels*, pp. 52, 110, 138–39, 151–52.

13. Thomas Edward Bowdich, *Mission from Cape Coast Castle to Ashantee* (London, 1819), pp. 198–99; John Duncan, *Travels in Western Africa in 1845 and 1846*, 2 vols. (London, 1847), I, 238–39. Park, *Travels*, pp. 26–27, 39–42.

14. Bowdich, *Mission*, pp. 36–44; cf. Duncan, *Travels*, I, 225–40.

15. Duncan, *Travels*, I, 225; see also Bowdich, *Mission*, p. 65.

16. Bowdich, *Mission*, p. 60.

17. Robert A. Lystad, *The Ashanti: A Proud People* (New Brunswick, New Jersey, 1958), pp. 27–28.

18. Duncan, *Travels*, I, 292.

19. Laing, *Travels*, p. 154.

20. Bowdich, *Mission*, pp. 212–25.

21. Duncan, *Travels*, I, 51–54.

22. Samuel Crowther, *Journal of an Expedition up the Niger and Tshadda Rivers* (London, 1855), pp. 128–29.

23. R. Lander in Clapperton, *Journal*, I, 152.

24. Macgregor Laird and R. A. K. Oldfield, *Narrative of an Expedition in the Interior of Africa by the River Niger in 1832–34*, 2 vols. (London, 1837), II, 56.

25. F. Harrison Rankin, *The White Man's Grave: A Visit to Sierra Leone in 1834*, 2 vols. (London, 1836).

The Golden Land: South Africa, 1800–1850

1. John Barrow, *Travels into the Interior of Southern Africa*, 2 vols. (London, 1806), II, 99.

2. *Ibid.*, I, 93–94.

3. *Ibid.*, I, 158–59.

4. Andrew Steedman, *Wanderings and Adventures in the Interior of Southern Africa*, 2 vols. (London, 1910), II, 136–37.

5. *Ibid.*, I, 171.

6. Robert Moffat, *Missionary Labours* (New York, 1842), p. 4.

7. John Campbell, *Travels in South Africa* (Andover, Massachusetts, 1916), p. 262.

8. David Livingstone, *Missionary Travels and Researches in South Africa* (New York, 1859), p. 34.

9. *Ibid.*, p. 47.

10. E.g., Moffat, *Labours;* Campbell, *Travels;* Allen F. Gardiner, *Narrative of a Journey to the Zoolu Country* (London, 1836); Robert Moffat, *Matabele Journals*, 2 vols. (London, 1945; first edition, 1855).

11. Livingstone, *Missionary Travels*, p. 25.

12. *Ibid.*, pp. 21–22.

13. *Ibid.*, pp. 549–50.

14. David Livingstone, *The Last Journals of David Livingstone in Central Africa from 1865 to his Death* (New York, 1875).

15. Douglas Woodruff, "Expansion and Emigration in Early Victorian England" in G. M. Young (ed.), *Early Victorian England* (London, 1934).

16. Thomas Pringle, *African Sketches* (London, 1834), p. 479.

17. Francis Galton, *Narrative of an Explorer in Tropical South Africa* (London, 1853), p. 189.

18. Alfred W. Cole, *The Cape and the Kaffirs* (London, 1852), p. 42; pp. 195ff.

19. Sir William Cornwallis Harris, *The Wild Sports of Southern Africa* (London, 1839), p. 346.

20. Moffat, *Labours*, p. 16.

21. Hugh Murray, Robert Jameson and James Wilson, *Narrative of Discovery and Adventure in Africa* (London, 1849), p. 301.

22. Henry M. Methuen, *Life in the Wilderness, or Wanderings in South Africa* (London, 1856), p. 35.

23. Harris, *Wild Sports of Southern Africa*, p. 65.

24. Livingstone, *Missionary Researches*, p. 69.

25. *Ibid.*, p. 69.

26. Captain Frederick Marryat, *The Mission, or Scenes in Africa* (London, 1845), p. 15.

Chapter II
The Saga of Exploration

1. Ronald Robinson, J. Gallagher and Alice Denny, *Africa and the Victorians, the Climax of Imperialism in the Dark Continent* (New York, 1961), pp. 15–16.

2. *Ibid.*, p. 16.

3. The Church Missionary Society in Uganda in 1877, and the London Missionary Society in Nyasa in 1878.

4. Sir Francis Burton, *The Lake Regions of Central Africa*, 2 vols. (New York, 1961; original edition, 1861), I, 145–57.

5. Alan Moorehead, *The White Nile* (New York, 1960), pp. 61–62.

6. John and Mrs. J. Petherick, *Travels in Central Africa and Explorations of the Western Nile Tributaries*, 2 vols. (London, 1869), II, Appendix A, 78–79.

7. W. E. Houghton, *The Victorian Frame of Mind, 1830–1870* (New Haven, 1957), p. 316.

8. Zoe Marsh, *East African History Through Contemporary Records* (Cambridge, 1961), p. 88.

9. John Hanning Speke, *Journey of the Discovery of the Source of the Nile* (New York, 1864), p. 513.

10. Sir Richard Francis Burton, *A Mission to Gelele, King of Dahomey*, 2 vols. (London, 1877), II, 44.

11. J. B. Thomson, *Joseph Thomson, African Explorer* (London, 1896), pp. 164–65.

12. Sir Samuel Baker, *Albert N'Yanza* (London, 1866), p. 445.

13. Verney Lovett Cameron, *Across Africa (1873–1876)* (New York, 1877), pp. 152–54.

14. Speke, *Journey*, Introduction, p. xxii.

15. David Livingstone, *Narrative of an Expedition to the Zambesi and its Tributaries: and of the discovery of the Lakes Shirwa and Nyassa, 1858–1864* (New York, 1866), p. 725.

16. Baker, *Albert N'Yanza*, "Introduction," p. xxii.

17. Henry M. Stanley, *In Darkest Africa, or the Quest, Rescue and Retreat of Emin, Governor of Equatoria*, 2 vols. (New York, 1890), I, 212 and 244.

18. Livingstone, *Last Journals*, p. 69.

19. J. B. Thomson, *Thomson*, p. 23.

20. Joseph Thomson, *To the Central African Lakes and Back*, 2 vols. (Boston, 1881; 2nd. ed.).

21. Joseph Thomson, *Through Masailand* (London, 1885), p. 574.

22. *Ibid.*, p. 574.

23. James Frederick Elton, *Journals of Travels and Researches among the Lakes and Mountains of Eastern and Central Africa*, edited and compiled by M. B. Cotterill (London, 1879), p. 155.

24. Thomson, *Masailand*, p. 503.

25. Henry M. Stanley, *How I Found Livingtone*, 2 vols. (New York, 1890), I, 311.

26. Baker, *Albert N'Yanza,* p. 297.

27. *Ibid.,* p. 298.

28. Stanley, *How I found Livingstone,* I, 336.

29. Speke, *Journey,* p. 335.

30. *Ibid.,* p. 335.

31. Burton, *Mission to Gelele,* II, 106.

32. Baker, *Albert N'Yanza,* p. 183.

The Setting of the Saga

1. Burton, *Lake Regions,* I, 91–92.

2. Stanley, *Darkest Africa,* I, 282.

3. Thomson, *Masailand,* p. 201.

4. Baker, *Albert N'Yanza,* p. 280.

5. Petherick, *Travels,* II, 6.

6. Baker, *Albert N'Yanza,* p. 130.

7. Burton, *Mission to Gelele,* I, 156.

8. Thomson, *Masailand,* p. 413.

9. *Ibid.,* p. 474.

10. Burton, *Mission to Gelele,* II, 118–19.

11. *Ibid.,* I, 156.

12. Livingstone, *Zambesi,* p. 297; Burton, *Lake Regions,* I, 120.

13. Cameron, *Across Africa,* p. 89; Burton, *Mission to Gelele,* I, 100; Anna Hinderer, *Seventeen Years in the Yoruba Country* (London, 1872), p. 297; Winwood Reade, *African Sketchbooks,* 2 vols. (London, 1873), II, 115.

14. Baker, *Albert N'Yanza,* pp. 152–53.

15. Stanley, *Dark Continent,* pp. 56–63.

16. Burton, *Mission to Gelele,* I, 134–35.

17. Stanley, *Dark Continent,* pp. 17–18, and *passim.*

18. A. M. Mackay, *Mackay of Uganda* (New York, 1890), pp. vi ff.; Speke, *Journey,* chapters XII, XIII, XIV: Robert P. Ashe, *Two Kings of Uganda* (London, 1890).

Mid-Century Fiction and the Work of Winwood Reade

1. Margaret Dalziel, *Popular Fiction 100 Years Ago* (London, 1957); Amy Cruse, *The Victorians and Their Books* (London, 1935).

2. E.g., Charles Reade, *A Simpleton* (Boston and New York, n.d.; original edition, 1873). Reade lists in his introduction at least ten primary sources for his African material.

3. Captain Frederick Marryat, *The Privateersman* (Boston, 1866); Reade, *A Simpleton;* J. A. Skertchly, *Melinda, the Caboceer, or Sport*

in Ashanti (New York, 1876); Henry M. Stanley, *My Kalulu* (New York, 1874); Reade, *African Sketchbooks.*

4. Marryat, *The Privateersman,* pp. 52–53.

5. J. B. Thomson, *Thomson,* p. 191.

6. Reade, *African Sketchbooks,* I, 168.

7. Winwood W. Reade, *Savage Africa,* 2 vols. (New York, 1864), I, 375–82.

8. Reade, *African Sketchbooks,* II, 359.

9. *Ibid.,* I, 55.

10. Reade, *African Sketchbooks,* I, 220–21, 223–25.

11. Reade, *Savage Africa,* I, 440; *African Sketchbooks,* II, 134–35.

12. Reade, *Savage Africa,* I, 454; *African Sketchbooks,* I, 309–19.

13. Reade, *Savage Africa,* I, 159–64, 398; II, 403, 426, 446.

14. Reade, *African Sketchbooks,* I, 223.

15. *Ibid.,* II, 306.

16. Burton, *Lake Regions,* II, 292.

17. Reade, *Savage Africa,* I, 249–50.

18. *Ibid.,* I, 383.

19. *Ibid.,* preface.

20. *Ibid.,* II, 451.

Chapter III
The Bearers of the Burden

1. J. R. Seeley, *The Expansion of England* (London, 1931); Sir Charles Dilke, *The British Empire* (London, 1899); James Bryce, *Impressions of South Africa* (New York, 1897); Rayne Kruger, *Goodbye, Dolly Gray; the Story of the Boer War* (London, 1959).

2. Seeley, *The Expansion of England,* p. 10.

3. Frederick D. Lugard, *The Rise of Our East African Empire,* 2 vols. (Edinburgh and London, 1893), I, 284; see also Alfred J. Swann, *Fighting the Slave Hunters in Central Africa* (London, 1910), pp. 314–15; F. Courtenay Selous, *Travel and Adventure in South East Africa* (London, 1893), p. 325; Thomas Alldridge, *A Transformed Colony, Sierra Leone, As it was and as it is. . . .* (London, 1910), pp. 122, 282.

4. Ewart S. Grogan and Arthur H. Sharp, *From the Cape to Cairo* (London, 1900).

5. Dorothy Wellesley, *Sir George Goldie, Founder of Nigeria* (London, 1934), ix.

6. Winston S. Churchill, *My African Journey* (London, 1908), p. 24.

7. Grogan, *Cape to Cairo*, p. 96.

8. J. B. Thomson, *Thomson*, p. 271.

9. F. Lugard, *Rise of East African Empire*, I, p. 243. See also E. J. Glave, *In Savage Africa; or Six Years of Adventure in Congoland* (New York, 1892), p. 16; and Swann, *Fighting the Slave Hunters*, p. 45.

10. J. Bryce, *Impressions of South Africa*, p. 240; see also Seymour Vandeleur, *Campaigning on the Upper Nile and Niger* (London, 1898), p. 25.

11. Swann, *Fighting the Slave Hunters*, pp. 203–4.

12. Basil Worsfold, *A History of South Africa* (London, 1900), pp. 41–44; Bryce, *Impressions*, pp. 390ff.

13. Grogan, *Cape to Cairo*, p. 324; Lionel Declé, *Three Years in Savage Africa* (London, 1898), p. 203; Sir Harry Johnston, *The River Congo, from its mouth to Bolobo* (London, 1884), pp. 70–71; Worsfold, *History*, p. 41.

14. Lugard, *Rise of East African Empire*, I, 84.

15. Grogan, *Cape to Cairo*, p. 231.

16. H. Rider Haggard, *Cetywayo and His White Neighbours* (London, 1882), p. 35; see also Sir Harry Johnston, *The Story of My Life* (New York, 1923), p. 237.

17. Lugard, *Rise of East African Empire*, I, 301.

18. Sir Harry Johnston, *British Central Africa* (New York, 1897), p. 68; see also W. Churchill, *African Journey*, pp. 43–48; Mrs. M. A. Pringle, *Towards the Mountains of the Moon* (London, 1883), p. 220; Declé, *Three Years*, pp. 125, 185–86; Mary Hall, *A Woman's Trek from the Cape to Cairo* (London, 1907), p. 300.

19. Swann, *Fighting the Slave Hunters*, p. 133; Declé, *Three Years*, pp. 29–31; Sir H. H. Johnston, *The Uganda Protectorate*, 2 vols. (London, 1902), I, 230–31.

20. Johnston, *British Central Africa*, pp. 68–69; Swann, *Fighting the Slave Hunters*, pp. 138–43.

21. Seeley, *Expansion*, p. 225; see also Sir Harry H. Johnston, *The Kilimanjaro Expedition* (London, 1886), p. 508.

22. Churchill, *African Journey*, p. 121.

23. Lugard, *Rise of East African Empire*, I, 204, 462–63.

24. Churchill, *African Journey*, pp. 54–55; Lugard, *Rise of East African Empire*, I, 488; Declé, *Three Years*, p. 369.

25. Ashe, *Two Kings of Uganda*, p. 124.

26. Worsfold, *History*, p. 98.

27. Bryce, *Impressions*, p. 526; Alice Blanche Balfour, *Twelve Hundred Miles in a Waggon* (London, 1895), p. 79; Constance

Larymore, *A Resident's Wife in Nigeria* (London, 1908), Chapter II.

28. Pringle, *Mountains of the Moon*, p. 233.

29. Hall, *Woman's Trek*, p. 231.

30. Mary Kingsley, *Travels in West Africa* (London, 1898), pp. 477–78.

31. Declé, *Three Years*, pp. 136–37.

32. Lady Flora Lugard, *A Tropical Dependency* (London, 1905).

33. Larymore, *Resident's Wife*, pp. 105, 215; see also Lady Florence Dixie, *In the Land of Misfortune* (London, 1882), pp. 109, 130.

34. Declé, *Three Years*, p. 339.

35. Larymore, *Resident's Wife*, p. 14.

The White Man's Burden

1. Johnston, *Uganda*, I, 85–86.

2. Alldridge, *Transformed Colony*, p. 97.

3. W. Churchill, *African Journey*, p. 208.

4. Kingsley, *Travels*, p. 11.

5. Hall, *Woman's Trek*, p. 21.

6. Ashe, *Two Kings of Uganda*, p. 182.

7. Arthur S. White, *The Development of Africa* (London, 1890), pp. 9, 238, 241; Churchill, *African Journey*, pp. 76–79; Johnston, *Uganda*, I, 77–78; Lugard, *Rise of East African Empire*, I, 506–8.

8. Churchill, *African Journey*, pp. 5, 8, 31.

9. Bryce, *Impressions*, pp. 43–44.

10. Johnston, *Uganda*, I, 88.

11. Worsfold, *History*, p. 125.

12. Vandeleur, *Campaigning*, p. 189; see also Johnston, *Kilimanjaro*, pp. 99–100; Selous, *Travel*, p. 346; Swann, *Fighting the Slave Hunters*, pp. 314–15; MacDonald, *Soldiering*, p. 195; Dixie, *Land of Misfortune*, p. 147; Grogan, *Cape to Cairo*, p. 224; Haggard, *Cetywayo*, p. 20; Charles H. Robinson, *Hausaland* (London, 1896), p. 274.

13. Lugard, *Rise of East African Empire*, II, 249–50.

14. *Ibid.*, I, 382.

15. Hall, *Woman's Trek*, pp. 28, 41, 111, 207, 238, 242, 251, 271.

16. Lugard described the Kikuyu (*Rise of East African Empire*, I, 327) as "honest, straightforward, intelligent, good-mannered and friendly." MacDonald (*Soldiering*, pp. 109, 111) asserted that Lugard had been completely misguided in his judgment of the Kikuyu and that they were "really excitable, treacherous, addicted to drink and utter scoundrels."

17. White, *Development of Africa*, pp. 105, 107, 122.

18. Lugard, *Rise of East African Empire*, I, 478–79.

19. Johnston, *Uganda*, II, 647; Churchill, *African Journey*, p. 106.

20. Vandeleur, *Campaigning*, p. 170.

21. Charles H. Robinson, *Nigeria, Our Latest Protectorate* (New York, 1900), pp. 7, 27.

22. Lugard, *Rise of East African Empire*, I, 400.

23. Kingsley, *Travels*, p. 24.

24. Lady Flora Lugard, *A Tropical Dependency*, pp. 21ff.

25. Grogan, *Cape to Cairo*, pp. 149–54.

26. E. E. Evans-Pritchard, "Zande Cannibalism," *Journal of the Royal Anthropological Institute*, 1960; L. and P. Bohannan, *The Tiv* (London, 1953).

27. Johnston, *British Central Africa*, pp. 394–96.

28. Bryce, *Impressions*, p. 359.

29. Johnston, *British Central Africa*, p. 408.

30. All the characteristics are not mentioned by all the writers, but they all mention at least some. Limitations of space do not permit page references for each of the attributions, but, for example, Bryce mentions most of them on pp. 92, 122, 356, 364, 387, 476 (*Impressions*).

31. Bryce, *Impressions*, p. 94; see also Lugard, *Rise*, I, 171.

32. Grogan, *Cape to Cairo*, p. 165; see also Declé, *Three Years*, p. 26; Selous, *Travel*, p. 95; Johnston, *Uganda*, I, 193.

33. Kingsley, *Travels*, p. 488.

34. Bryce, *Impressions*, p. 375; see also Worsfold, *History*, p. 61; Swann, *Fighting the Slave Hunters*, pp. 330–34; Johnston, *British Central Africa*, pp. 202–6; Selous, *Travel*, p. 135.

35. Declé, *Three Years*, p. 5.

36. Vandeleur, *Campaigning*, pp. 161–62.

37. Johnston, *British Central Africa*, pp. 184, 202–3; Bryce, *Impressions*, p. 382; Kingsley, *Travels*, pp. 502–3.

38. Johnston, *Congo*, pp. 8 and 26, and *British Central Africa*, p. 19.

Fiction of Empire

1. Winifred Hall, *The Overseas Empire in Fiction* (London, 1942); Susan Howe, *Novels of Empire* (New York, 1949); William Y. Tindall, *Forces in Modern British Literature, 1885–1946* (New York, 1947).

2. Morton N. Cohen, *Rider Haggard, His Life and Works* (New York, 1960), p. 96.

3. G. A. Henty, *Young Colonists* (New York, n.d.; original edition, 1888).

4. In recent years there has been a small revival of Henty's novels.

His books are being bought up by the toy soldier *aficionados,* to re-enact the battle scenes.

5. Sir Percy Fitzpatrick, *Jock of the Bushveld* (London, 1907).

6. John Buchan, *Prester John* (Boston, 1928; original edition, 1910).

7. Sir Rider Haggard, *Three Novels of Adventure* (New York, 1953).

8. John Chalmers, *Fighting the Matabele* (London, 1898); Sir Bertram Mitford, *The King's Assegai* (London, 1895); Fitzpatrick, *Jock of the Bushveld;* Henty, *Young Colonists.*

9. Mary Gaunt, *The Uncounted Cost* (London, 1904); Sir Bertram Mitford, *John Ames, Native Commissioner* (London, 1900); Ernest Glanville, *The Fossicker* (London, 1891); H. R. Haggard, *Jess* (New York, 1890).

10. Cohen, *Rider Haggard,* p. 113.

11. Mitford, *King's Assegai.*

12. Mitford, *John Ames;* Chalmers, *Matabele;* Glanville, *The Fossickers.*

13. Rudyard Kipling, "The Captive," "A Sahib's War," "Comprehension of Private Cooper," in *Traffics and Discoveries* (New York, 1927; original edition, 1904), also "Egypt of the Magicians", in *Letters of Travel, 1892–1913* (New York, 1927; original edition, 1914).

14. Edgar Wallace, *Sanders of the River* (Garden City, 1930; original edition, 1909).

15. W. Somerset Maugham, *The Explorer* (New York, 1907), p. 180.

16. *Ibid.,* p. 279.

17. *Ibid.,* p. 178.

18. Buchan, *Prester John,* p. 264.

19. Rudyard Kipling, *Something of Myself* (New York, 1937).

20. Olive Schreiner, *The Story of an African Farm* (New York, n.d.; original edition, 1895).

21. *Ibid.,* p. 52.

22. *Ibid.,* p. 170.

23. Joseph Conrad, *Heart of Darkness* (New York, 1961; original edition, 1899) and "An Outpost of Progress," *Tales of Unrest* (New York, 1925; original edition, 1898).

24. Conrad, *Heart of Darkness,* p. 16.

25. *Ibid.,* p. 17.

26. *Ibid.,* p. 18.

27. *Ibid.,* p. 50.

28. Wallace, *Sanders of the River,* p. 277.

29. Conrad, "Outpost of Progress," p. 130.

30. Fitzpatrick, *Jock of the Bushveld*, p. 17.

31. Maugham, *Explorer*, p. 277; see also p. 45.

32. Mitford, *John Ames*, p. 86; see also Chalmers, *Matabele*, pp. 116–17; Buchan, *Prester John*, p. 139; Fitzpatrick, *Jock of the Bushveld*, p. 199; Maugham, *Explorer*, p. 160.

33. Cohen, *Rider Haggard*, p. 21.

34. Conrad, "Outpost of Progress," p. 132.

35. Mitford, *John Ames*, p. 5.

36. Fitzpatrick, *Jock of the Bushveld*, p. 207.

37. Glanville, *Fossicker*, p. 123.

38. Chalmers, *Matabele*, pp. 49–56.

39. William Charles Scully, *Kaffir Stories* (London, 1895).

40. H. Rider Haggard, *Nada the Lily* (London, 1892).

41. Buchan, *Prester John*, p. 201.

42. Fitzpatrick, *Jock of the Bushveld*, p. 197.

43. Haggard, *Allan Quatermain*, p. 430.

44. Buchan, *Prester John*, p. 201.

45. Haggard, *Allan Quatermain*, p. 458.

46. Fitzpatrick, *Jock of the Bushveld*, pp. 167–68.

Chapter IV
The Tradition in the Twentieth Century

1. D. W. Brogan, *The English People—Impressions and Observations* (New York, 1943), pp. 7–8; footnote, p. 8; Rayne Kruger, *Good-bye, Dolly Grey, The Story of the Boer War* (London, 1959), pp. 144ff.; A. Conan Doyle, *The Boer War* (New York, 1900).

2. Calvin Stillman (ed.), *Africa in the Modern World* (Chicago, 1955), pp. 289–90.

3. John Buchan, *Island of Sheep* (London, 1960), pp. 64–65.

4. Buchan, *Prester John*, p. 188.

5. Reginald Coupland, *Kirk of the Zambesi* (Oxford, 1928); Stephen Gwyn, *The Life of Mary Kingsley* (London, 1932); Elspeth Huxley, *White Man's Country*, 2 vols. (London, 1935); Margery Perham, *Lugard*, 2 vols. (London, 1960); Dorothy Wellesley, *Sir George Goldie, Founder of Nigeria* (London, 1934).

6. Ian Henderson, *Man-Hunt in Kenya* (Garden City, 1958).

7. Sir Charles Dundas, *African Crossroads* (London, 1955), p. 143.

8. Peter Viertel, *White Hunter, Black Heart* (London, 1954), p. 18.

9. Winifred Holtby, *Mandoa, Mandoa!* (New York, 1933); Gwyn Griffin, *By the North Gate* (New York, 1959), and *Something of an*

Achievement (New York, 1960); Evelyn Waugh, *Black Mischief* (New York, 1960).

10. Alan Scholefield, *A View of Vultures* (London, 1966), and *Great Elephant* (New York, 1968).

11. Eric Ambler, *Dirty Story* (New York, 1967); June Drummond, *Welcome, Proud Lady* (New York, 1968); Shirley Milne, *Beware the Lurking Scorpion* (New York, 1966).

12. Dr. Grantly Dick Read, *No Time for Fear* (New York, 1955), p. 204.

13. Stuart Cloete, *The African Giant* (Boston, 1955), pp. 290–91.

Chapter V
The Abysmal Gulf

1. Laurens Van der Post, *The Dark Eye in Africa* (New York, 1955), p. 43.

2. Max Catto, *Gold in the Sky* (New York, 1958), pp. 9–10.

3. Richard Wyndham, *The Gentle Savage* (New York, 1936), p. 47.

4. Elspeth Huxley, *The Walled City* (Philadelphia, 1949), p. 176.

5. Joy Packer, *The Glass Barrier* (Philadelphia, 1961), p. 254; see also Harold Bindloss, *The League of the Leopard* (London, 1923), p. 155; Harry Bloom, *Whittaker's Wife* (New York, 1962), p. 36; Gerald Hanley, *The Year of the Lion* (New York, 1954), p. 89; Llewelyn Powys, *Ebony and Ivory* (New York, 1923), p. 40; William Plomer, *Double Lives* (New York, 1956), pp. 107, 156; Laurens Van der Post, *Venture to the Interior* (New York, 1951), p. 102.

6. Cloete, *Giant*, p. 327.

7. Joy Packer, *Apes and Ivory* (London, 1953), p. 204.

8. Elspeth Huxley, *The Flame Trees of Thika* (New York, 1959), p. 67.

9. Robert Lait, *Honey for Tomorrow* (New York, 1961), p. 149.

10. William C. Scully, *Further Reminiscences of a South African Pioneer* (London, 1913), p. 252.

11. John Rowan Wilson, *Double Blind* (Garden City, 1960), p. 283.

12. Augustus C. Collodon, *Congo Jake* (New York, 1933), pp. 212–213.

13. Isak Dinesen, *Out of Africa* (New York, 1938), pp. 134–35.

14. Graham Greene, *Journey Without Maps* (New York, 1961), pp. 36–40.

15. Nicholas Monsarrat, *The Tribe that Lost Its Head* (New York, 1956), pp. 517–18.

16. Raymond Tong, *Figures in Ebony* (London, 1958), p. 86.

17. Greene, *Journey Without Maps,* p. 50.

18. Joyce Cary, *The Case for African Freedom* (London, 1944), pp. 39–40.

Chapter VI
The Dark Labyrinth

1. Elspeth Huxley, *Four Guineas* (London, 1954), p. 292.

2. Greene, *Journey Without Maps,* p. 46.

3. Graham Greene, *In Search of a Character* (New York, 1961), p. 93.

4. Cullen Gouldsbury, *An African Year* (London, 1912), p. 128.

5. Lady Dorothy Mills, *The Golden Land* (London, 1926), p. 13.

6. Tong, *Figures in Ebony,* pp. 28–29; see also, Mills, *Golden Land,* pp. 14, 170.

7. Catto, *Gold in the Sky,* p. 167.

8. Monsarrat, *The Tribe that Lost Its Head,* p. 12.

9. Wyndham, *The Gentle Savage,* p. 125.

10. Cloete, *Giant,* p. 110; see also p. 256.

11. Holtby, *Mandoa, Mandoa!,* p. 163.

12. Cloete, *Giant,* p. 376; see also Joyce Cary, *Aissa Saved* (London, 1952), p. 8; Elspeth Huxley, *On the Edge of the Rift* (New York, 1962), p. 269; Bloom, *Whittaker's Wife,* pp. 174–75.

13. Ronald Hardy, *The Men from the Bush* (Garden City, 1959), p. 84.

14. Talbot Mundy, *The Ivory Trail* (Indianapolis, 1919), p. 76.

15. Griffin, *By the North Gate,* p. 116.

16. Huxley, *Four Guineas,* p. 175.

17. Max Catto, *Mr. Moses* (New York, 1961), p. 30; *Gold in the Sky,* p. 100.

18. Collodon, *Congo Jake,* p. viii; Catto, *Gold in the Sky,* p. 34; Gerald Hanley, *Drinkers of Darkness* (New York, 1955), pp. 129, 164.

19. Elspeth Huxley, *The Red Rock Wilderness* (New York, 1957), pp. 236–37.

20. Hanley, *Drinkers of Darkness,* pp. 164–65; see also Gerald Hanley, *Gilligan's Last Elephant* (Cleveland, 1962), p. 74; Lady Dorothy Mills, *Road to Timbuktu* (London, 1924), p. 251; Mary Motley, *Devils in Waiting* (London, 1959), pp. 138–41; Robert Shaw, *The Sun Doctor* (New York, 1961), p. 90; Marguerite Steen, *Twilight on the Floods* (Garden City, 1949), pp. 357–58; Tong, *Figures in Ebony,* p. 96.

21. Greene, *Journey Without Maps*, pp. 11 and 33.

22. Laurens Van der Post, *The Heart of the Hunter* (New York, 1961), p. xiv; see also Hanley, *Drinkers of Darkness*, p. 33.

23. Alan Moorehead, *The White Nile* (New York, 1960), pp. 116–117; see also Thomas Sterling, *Stanley's Way* (New York, 1960). This American chronicler of Stanley's journeys gives a parallel interpretation of Stanley. Far from being the indomitable explorer, he views Stanley as the eternal lost boy searching for a father.

24. Powys, *Ebony and Ivory*, pp. 22–23.

25. Greene, *Journey Without Maps*, p. 114; see also Van der Post, *The Dark Eye in Africa*, p. 81.

26. Van der Post, *Venture to the Interior*, p. 198.

27. Van der Post, *Dark Eye in Africa*, p. 250.

28. *Ibid.*, pp. 55–56.

Chapter VII
The Strange Woman

1. Marguerite Steen, *The Sun Is My Undoing* (New York, 1941), p. 319.

2. Margery Perham and Jack Simmons, *African Discovery* (London, 1948), p. 5.

3. Steen, *Twilight on the Floods*, p. 358.

4. Stuart Cloete, *Congo Song* (New York, 1958), p. 97.

5. Cloete, *Giant*, p. 51.

6. Joyce Cary, *Mr. Johnson* (New York, 1961), p. 170.

7. Edwin W. Smith and Andrew Dale, *The Ila-Speaking Peoples of Northern Rhodesia* (London, 1920), pp. 48–49.

8. *Ibid.*, p. 67.

9. John Seymour, *One Man's Africa* (New York, 1956), p. 218.

10. Dinesen, *Out of Africa*, p. 125.

11. Shaw, *The Sun Doctor*, p. 30.

12. Hanley, *Drinkers of Darkness*, p. 57.

13. Cloete, *Giant*, p. 316.

14. Hanley, *Drinkers of Darkness*, p. 55.

15. Hanley, *Gilligan's Last Elephant*, p. 108.

16. Mills, *The Golden Land*, p. 51.

17. Ian Brook, *Jimmy Riddle* (New York, 1961); Richard Llewellyn, *A Man in a Mirror* (New York, 1961).

Chapter VIII
The Land in Amber

1. Hanley, *The Year of the Lion,* p. 176.
2. Huxley, *On the Edge of the Rift,* p. 54.
3. Van der Post, *Venture to the Interior,* p. 294.
4. Huxley, *Walled City,* p. 172.
5. Van der Post, *The Heart of the Hunter,* p. 80.
6. Viertel, *White Hunter,* p. 76.
7. Hanley, *The Year of the Lion,* p. 22.
8. Isak Dinesen, *Shadows on the Grass* (New York, 1961), p. 3.
9. Robert Henriques, *Death by Moonlight* (New York, 1938), p. 220.
10. Elspeth Huxley, *A New Earth* (New York, 1960), p. 66.
11. Griffin, *Something of an Achievement,* pp. 132–33.
12. Lord Vansittart, "Foreword" to H. C. Jackson, *Sudan Days and Ways* (London, 1954).
13. Lord Cranworth, *Kenya Chronicles* (London, 1939), p. 37.
14. A. C. G. Hastings, *Nigerian Days* (London, 1925), p. 77.
15. H. Rider Haggard, *The Days of My Life,* 2 vols. (London, 1926), I, 202.
16. Dinesen, *Shadows on the Grass,* pp. 8–9.
17. Read, *No Time for Fear,* p. 212.
18. Cary, *The Case for African Freedom,* p. 44.
19. Roderick Cameron, *Equator Farm* (New York, 1956), p. 164.
20. *Ibid.,* p. 45.
21. C. W. Hobley, *Kenya from Chartered Company to Crown Colony* (London, 1929).
22. Melville J. Herskovits, *The Human Factor in Changing Africa* (New York, 1962), pp. 82, 477.
23. Cameron, *Equator Farm,* pp. 125–26.
24. Huxley, *Flame Trees of Thika,* p. 116.

Chapter IX
The Antagonist

1. Perham and Simmons, *African Discovery,* p. 15.
2. Huxley, *Red Rock Wilderness,* p. 134.
3. Monsarrat, *The Tribe that Lost Its Head,* p. 120.
4. Van der Post, *Dark Eye in Africa,* pp. 44–45.
5. Greene, *Journey Without Maps,* p. 175.

6. Catto, *Gold in the Sky* and *Mr. Moses;* Stuart Cloete, *Gazella* (New York, 1959), and *Congo Song;* C. S. Forester, *The African Queen* (New York, 1960); Holtby, *Mandoa, Mandoa!;* Huxley, *Red Rock Wilderness;* Monsarrat, *The Tribe that Lost Its Head;* Waugh, *Black Mischief.*

7. Greene, *In Search of a Character,* p. 17.

8. Catto, *Gold in the Sky,* pp. 118–19.

9. Cloete, *Gazella,* pp. 108–9.

10. Dundas, *Crossroads,* pp. 58–59.

11. Alastair Scobie, *Women of Africa* (London, 1960), p. 173.

12. Dundas, *Crossroads,* p. 59.

13. Hanley, *Year of the Lion,* p. 192.

14. Wilson, *Double Blind,* p. 70.

15. Steen, *Twilight on the Floods,* p. 301.

16. Hardy, *Men from the Bush,* p. 108.

17. Beryl Markham, *West with the Night* (Boston, 1942), p. 60.

18. Van der Post, *Venture to the Interior,* p. 93.

19. Elspeth Huxley, *The Sorcerer's Apprentice* (London, 1949), p. 43.

20. Donald L. Wiedner, *A History of Africa* (New York, 1962), p. 11.

21. Cary, *Case for African Freedom,* p. 136.

22. Hanley, *Year of the Lion,* p. 177.

23. Tom Stacey, *The Brothers M* (New York, 1961), p. 11.

24. Hanley, *Drinkers of Darkness,* p. 77.

25. Basil Davidson, *The Lost Cities of Africa* (Boston, 1957), p. 65.

26. *Ibid.,* p. viii.

27. Cloete, *Giant,* p. 368.

28. Huxley, *Walled City,* p. 168.

29. Julian Mockford, *Golden Land* (London, 1949), p. 99.

30. Van der Post, *Dark Eye in Africa,* p. 62.

31. Catto, *Mr. Moses,* p. 8.

32. Dundas, *Crossroads,* p. 242.

33. Joyce Cary, *The African Witch* (London, 1951), p. 12.

34. Lait, *Honey for Tomorrow,* p. 162.

35. Packer, *Apes and Ivory,* p. 298.

36. Huxley, *Red Rock Wilderness,* p. 110.

37. Wellesley, *Sir George Goldie,* pp. 150–51.

Chapter X
The British Self-Image

1. Hilaire Belloc, *An Essay on the Nature of Contemporary England* (New York, 1937), p. 26; see also pp. 28, 29.

2. James Wellard, *Understanding the English* (New York, 1937), p. 90.

3. Philip Carr, *The English Are Like That* (New York, 1941), p. 134.

4. J. D. Scott, *Life in Britain* (New York, 1955), p. 10; see also Harold Nicolson, *Good Behaviour* (Garden City, 1956), p. 250; Roy Lewis and Angus Maude, *Professional People in England* (Cambridge, 1953), p. 263.

5. George Orwell, *A Collection of Essays* (Garden City, 1954), p. 274.

6. Martin Green, *A Mirror for Anglo-Saxons: A discovery of America, a rediscovery of England* (New York, 1960), p. 78.

7. Nicolson, *Good Behaviour*, p. 262.

8. Green, *A Mirror for Anglo-Saxons*, p. 123; Orwell, *Essays*, p. 261; Wellard, *Understanding the English*, pp. 11, 43, 96, 106, 157.

9. G. D. H. Cole, *The Post-War Condition of Britain* (London, 1956), p. 26; T. H. Pear, *English Social Differences* (London, 1955); David C. Marsh, *The Changing Social Structure of England and Wales, 1871–1951* (London, 1958); Nancy Mitford, *Noblesse Oblige* (New York, 1956).

10. Green, *A Mirror for Anglo-Saxons*, p. 51.

11. Pear, *Social Differences*, p. 60.

12. Geoffrey Gorer, *Exploring English Character* (New York, 1955), p. 2.

13. B. M. Spinley, *The Deprived and the Privileged: Personality Development in English Society* (London, 1953).

14. Gorer, *Exploring English Character*, p. 2.

15. *Ibid.*, p. 163.

16. *Ibid.*, p. 13; see also Margaret Mead, *The Application of Anthropological Techniques to Cross-National Communication* (New York, 1947), p. 136; Scott, *Life in Britain*, pp. 19–20; Spinley, *The Deprived and the Privileged*, p. 104; Martha Wolfenstein and Nathan Leites, *Movies* (Glencoe, 1950), p. 295.

17. Gorer, *Exploring English Character*, p. 288.

18. Scott, *Life in Britain*, p. 20.

19. Gorer, *Exploring English Character*, pp. 289–91.

20. Carr, *The English Are Like That,* p. 265.

21. *Ibid.,* p. 265.

22. *Ibid.,* p. 19.

23. *Ibid.,* p. 19; see also Denis W. Brogan, *The English People—Impressions and Observations* (New York, 1943), pp. 144, 285; Pear, *Social Differences,* p. 176; Wellard, *Understanding the English,* p. 76.

24. Carr, *The English Are Like That,* p. 74; see also p. 81; Norman Dennis, Fernando Henriques and Clifford Slaughter, *Coal Is Our Life* (London, 1956), p. 218; Gorer, *Exploring English Character,* pp. 75, 76; Scott, *Life in Britain,* pp. 16–17.

25. Dennis, Henriques and Slaughter, *Coal Is Our Life,* p. 211.

26. Gorer, *Exploring English Character,* p. 75.

27. *Ibid.,* p. 303; Spinley, *The Deprived and the Privileged,* p. 136; Wellard, *Understanding the English,* p. 53.

28. Dennis, Henriques and Slaughter, *Coal Is Our Life,* p. 226.

29. *Ibid.,* p. 231.

30. Wellard, *Understanding the English,* p. 54.

31. R. F. L. Logan and E. M. Goldberg, "Rising Eighteen in a London Suburb," *British Journal of Sociology,* IV, 333; Eliot Slater and Moya Woodside, *Patterns of Marriage* (London, 1951), p. 167.

32. Slater and Woodside, *Patterns of Marriage,* p. 167.

33. Scott, *Life in Britain,* p. 15.

34. Gorer, *Exploring English Character,* p. 287.

35. Green, *Mirror for Anglo-Saxons,* pp. 31–32.

36. David Victor Glass (ed.), *Social Mobility in Britain* (Glencoe, 1954), pp. 177–217.

37. Cole, *Post-War Condition of Britain,* p. 38.

38. Lewis and Maude, *Professional People,* p. 220.

39. Pear, *Social Differences,* p. 152.

40. Brogan, *The English People,* p. 254.

41. Orwell, *Essays,* p. 278.

42. John Strachey, *The End of Empire* (New York, 1960), p. 204.

43. Brogan, *The English People,* p. 5.

44. David Frost and Anthony Jay, *The English* (New York, 1968), p. 57.

45. K. B. Smellie, *The British Way of Life* (London, 1955), p. 148.

46. Gorer, *Exploring English Character,* p. 117.

47. Brogan, *The English People,* pp. 82, 83, 101, 103, 106; Dennis, Henriques and Slaughter, *Coal Is Our Life,* p. 169; Lewis and Maude, *Professional People,* pp. 138, 141, 264; Marsh, *Social Structure,* pp. 188, 189; Orwell, *Essays,* p. 241; Slater and Woodside, *Patterns of Marriage,* pp. 124, 193, 256, 260; Smellie, *British Way of Life,* p. 48;

B. S. Rowntree and G. R. Lavers, *English Life and Leisure* (London, 1951), Chapter XIII.

48. George Orwell, *The Road to Wigan Pier* (New York, 1961), p. 162.

49. *Ibid.*, p. 175.

50. Frost and Jay, *The English,* pp. 254–55.

bibliography

BACKGROUND

The background materials include critical biographies, African history and anthropology, and other studies of the Western view of alien people. The works listed are selective; those which were directly pertinent and to which we had immediate reference. Ideally, such a bibliography should be limitless, since there is almost no end to the literature which helped to formulate the ideas basic to this study. Many of the ideas are the ineluctable consequence of two lifetimes spent as anthropologists, and to document them would require listing most of the significant works in anthropology.

Annals of the American Academy of Political and Social Science. Sept. 1954.

BAINES, JOCELYN. *Joseph Conrad—A Critical Biography.* New York: McGraw-Hill, 1960.

BOHANNAN, LAURA and PAUL. *The Tiv of Central Nigeria. Ethnographic Survey of Africa,* Part VIII. London: International African Institute, 1953.

BOVILL, W. E. *The Golden Trade of the Moors.* London: Oxford University Press, 1958.

BRODIE, FAWN M. *The Devil Drives: A Life of Sir Richard Burton.* New York: W. W. Norton, 1967.

BURNS, SIR ALAN. *History of Nigeria.* London: Allen and Unwin, 1929.

CARRINGTON, JOHN F. *Talking Drums of Africa.* London: Kingsgate Press, 1949.

COHEN, MORTON N. *Rider Haggard: His Life and Works.* New York: Walker and Co., 1961.

COUPLAND, REGINALD. *Kirk on the Zambesi.* Oxford: Clarendon Press, 1928.

————. *The Exploitation of East Africa, 1856–1890: The Slave Trade and the Scramble.* London: Faber and Faber, 1939.

CURTIN, PHILIP D. *The Image of Africa.* Madison: The University of Wisconsin Press, 1964.

DAICHES, DAVID. *White Man in the Tropics: Two Moral Tales.* New York: Harcourt, Brace and World, Inc., 1962.

DAVIDSON, BASIL. *The Lost Cities of Africa.* Boston: Little, Brown and Co., 1957.

————. *Black Mother.* Boston: Little, Brown and Co., 1961.

DIKE, K. ONWUKA. *Trade and Politics on the Niger Delta, 1830–1885.* Oxford: Clarendon Press, 1956.

DRIVER, DAVID MILLER. *The Indian in Brazilian Literature.* New York: Hispanic Institute in the United States, 1942.

DYKES, E. B. *The Negro in English Romantic Thought.* Washington, 1942.

EVANS-PRITCHARD, E. E. "Zande Cannibalism," *Journal of the Royal Anthropological Institute,* 90, Pt. 2. 1960, 238–58.

FAGE, J. D. *An Introduction to the History of West Africa.* Cambridge: Cambridge University Press, 1961.

————. *Ghana—A Historical Interpretation.* Madison: University of Wisconsin Press, 1959.

FAIRCHILD, HOXIE N. *The Noble Savage: A Study in Romantic Naturalism.* New York: Columbia University Press, 1928.

GEORGE, KATHERINE. "The Civilized West Looks at Primitive Africa: 1400–1800." *Isis,* 49 (1958), 62–72.

GLUCKMAN, MAX. "The Kingdom of the Zulu of South Africa," in FORTES, M., and E. E. EVANS-PRITCHARD (eds.), *African Political Systems.* London: Oxford University Press for the International African Institute, 1940, 25–55.

GWYNN, STEPHEN. *Mungo Park.* New York: G. P. Putnam Sons, 1935.

————. *The Life of Mary Kingsley.* London: Macmillan, 1932.

HAINES, C. GROVE (ed.). *Africa Today.* Baltimore: Johns Hopkins University Press, 1955.

HAMMOND, DOROTHY. "The Image of Africa in the British Literature of the Twentieth Century," Ph.D. dissertation. University of Michigan Microfilm, 1963.

———— and ALTA JABLOW. "The African in Western Literature," *Africa Today,* Dec. 1960 and Jan. 1961.

HANKE, LEWIS. "Aristotle and the Indian," *Texas Quarterly,* Spring, 1958.

HENNESSEY, MAURICE. *The Congo—A Brief History and Appraisal.* New York: Frederick A. Praeger, 1961.

HERSKOVITS, MELVILLE J. *The Human Factor in Changing Africa.* New York: Alfred A. Knopf, 1962.

——. *Man and His Works.* New York: Alfred A. Knopf, 1949.

——. *Dahomey.* Vol. II. New York: J. J. Augustin, 1938.

HOBLEY, G. W. *Kenya from Chartered Company to Crown Colony.* London: H. F. and G. Witherby, 1929.

HODGKIN, THOMAS. *Nigerian Perspectives.* London: Oxford University Press, 1960.

HUXLEY, ELSPETH. *White Man's Country.* 2 vols. London: Macmillan Co., 1935.

ISAACS, HAROLD. *Scratches on Our Minds: American Images of China and India.* New York: John Day Co., 1958.

JABLOW, ALTA. "The Development of a Literary Tradition: The British in Africa, 1530–1910." Ph.D. dissertation. University of Michigan Microfilms, 1963.

KLINEBERG, OTTO. "Pictures in Our Heads," *UNESCO Courier,* 8, No. 4 (Sept. 1955), 5–9.

KRUGER, RAYNE. *Goodbye, Dolly Grey: The Story of the Boer War.* London: Cassell and Co., 1959.

LYSTAD, ROBERT A. *The Ashanti, A Proud People.* New Brunswick: Rutgers University Press, 1958.

MAHOOD, MOLLY M. *Joyce Cary's Africa.* London: Methuen, 1964.

MARSH, ZOE (ed.). *East African History Through Contemporary Records.* Cambridge: Cambridge University Press, 1961.

MERKER, M. *Die Masai.* Berlin: D. Reimer, 1904.

MERRIAM, ALAN P. "A Prologue to the Study of African Arts," *Antioch College Founder's Day Lectures.* No. 7. Yellow Springs: Antioch Press, 1961.

MOOREHEAD, ALAN. *The White Nile.* New York: Harper and Brothers, 1960.

——. *The Blue Nile.* New York: Harper and Row, 1962.

MPHAHLELE, EZEKIEL. *The African Image.* New York: Frederick A. Praeger, 1962.

PEARCE, ROY H. *The Savages of America.* Baltimore: Johns Hopkins University Press, 1953.

PEDRAZA, HOWARD J. *Borrioboola Gha: The Story of Lokoja, the First British Settlement in Nigeria.* London: Oxford University Press, 1960.

PERHAM, MARGERY. *Lugard.* 2 vols. London: Collins, 1960.

—— and JACK SIMMONS. *African Discovery.* London: Penguin Books, 1948.

POPE-HENNESSY, JAMES. *Sins of the Fathers: A Study of the Atlantic Slave Traders, 1441–1807.* New York: Knopf, 1968.

RATTRAY, ROBERT S. *Ashanti Law and Constitution.* London: Oxford University Press, 1929.

————. *Religion and Art in Ashanti.* London: Oxford University Press, 1927.

SCHNEIDER, HAROLD K. "Pakot Resistance to Change," in William Bascom and Melville J. Herskovits (eds.), *Continuity and Change in African Culture.* Chicago: University of Chicago Press, 1954.

SIMMONS, JACK. *Livingstone and Africa.* New York: Crowell, 1962.

SMITH, BERNARD. *European Vision and the South Pacific, 1768–1850.* London: Oxford University Press, 1960.

SMITH, EDWIN W. and ANDREW M. DALE. *The Ila-Speaking Peoples of Northern Rhodesia.* 2 vols. London: Macmillan, 1920.

STERLING, THOMAS. *Stanley's Way.* New York: Atheneum, 1960.

STILLMAN, CALVIN W. *Africa in the Modern World.* Chicago: University of Chicago Press, 1955.

SYPHER, WYLIE. *Guinea's Captive Kings: British Anti-Slavery Literature of the XVIII Century.* Chapel Hill: University of North Carolina Press, 1942.

WEISCHOFF, H. A. *Colonial Policies in Africa.* Philadelphia: University of Pennsylvania Press, 1944.

WELLESLEY, DOROTHY. *Sir George Goldie, Founder of Nigeria.* London: Macmillan, 1934.

WIEDNER, DONALD L. *A History of Africa South of the Sahara.* New York: Random House, 1962.

WOLFSON, FREDA. *Pageant of Ghana.* London: Oxford University Press, 1958.

WRIGHT, ANDREW. *Joyce Cary, A Preface to His Novels.* New York: Harper and Brothers, 1958.

THE BRITISH IN AFRICA: 1530–1910

The works listed below comprise the sources for the first half of this study. They contain the historical data and include primarily the journals of explorers, traders, settlers, officials, missionaries, and visitors; there are also some early compendia of travelers' accounts in the collections of Hakluyt, Purchas, Churchill, and Blake, and a few later books on the whole of Africa compiled by armchair commentators. We have, undoubtedly, omitted many items to which particular readers may be committed, but the sample is sufficient to indicate that even the exceptional work would scarcely change the over-all picture. Omissions were not intentional, save in a very few instances. For example, we deliberately did not include the great pioneer work of James Bruce, *Travels to Discover the Source of the Nile*, first published in 1790. He was, for us, an explorer in the wrong place at the wrong time, since his explorations in Ethiopia, and his concern with the Nile sources were well in advance of the mainstream of such activity on the part of the British. Ethiopia was, in any event, outside the major areas of British concern in Africa, and its culture differed greatly from the African cultures south of the Sahara. The British literature on Ethiopia merits separate study.

The bibliographic listings will follow the main chapter headings as far as possible. Some of the authors may be assigned to more than one chapter, since their lifetimes and interests range over several time periods and areas. In such cases we have separated their works for listing in the appropriate chapters. The fiction of this entire period is listed separately, and only those novels to which we have made direct reference are included in the bibliography.

Chapter I. First Light on the Dark Continent

ALLEN, CAPTAIN WILLIAM and T. R. H. THOMPSON. *Narrative of the Expedition to the River Niger in 1841.* 2 vols. London: Richard Bentley, 1848.

BAIKIE, WILLIAM BALFOUR. *Narrative of an Exploring Voyage up the Rivers Kwora and Binue in 1854.* London: John Murray, 1856.

BARNARD, LADY ANNE. *South Africa a Century Ago* ("Letters from the Cape of Good Hope: 1798–1801"). W. H. WILKINS (ed.). London: 1901.

BARROW, JOHN. *Travels into the Interior of Southern Africa.* 2 vols. 2nd ed. London: T. Cadell and W. Davies, 1806.

BEECHAM, JOHN. *Ashantee.* London: John Mason, 1841.

BLAKE, J. W. *Europeans in West Africa, 1450–1560.* Vol. II. London: Hakluyt Society, 1942.

BOWDICH, THOMAS EDWARD. *Mission from Cape Coast Castle to Ashantee, with a statistical account of that Kingdom, and geographical notices of other parts of the interior of Africa.* London: John Murray, 1819.

BURCHELL, W. J. *Travels in the Interior of Southern Africa.* 2 vols. London: Batchworth Press, 1949 (reprinted from the original edition of 1822).

CAMPBELL, JOHN. *Travels in South Africa.* Andover, Mass.: Flag and Gould, 1916.

CHURCHILL, J. *Collections of Travels and Voyages.* London: Vols. I–IV, 1704; V–VI, 1732.

CLAPPERTON, HUGH. *Journal of a Second Expedition into the Interior of Africa, and the Journal of Richard Lander*. Philadelphia: Lea and Corey, 1829.

COLE, ALFRED W. *The Cape and the Kafirs*. London: Richard Bentley, 1852.

COOLEY, WILLIAM D. *Inner Africa Laid Open*. London: Longman, Brown, Green and Longmans, 1852.

CROWTHER, SAMUEL. *Journal of an Expedition up the Niger and Tshadda Rivers*. London: Church Missionary House, 1855.

CRUICKSHANK, BRODIE. *Eighteen Years on the Gold Coast of Africa*. 2 vols. London: Hurst and Blackett, 1853.

DALZEL, ARCHIBALD. *The History of Dahomy, an inland kingdom of Africa, compiled from authentic memoirs*. London: T. Spilsbury, 1793.

DUNCAN, JOHN. *Travels in Western Africa in 1845 and 1846*. 2 vols. London: Richard Bentley, 1847.

FREEMAN, T. B. *Journals of Various Visits to the Kingdom of Ashanti*. London, 1844.

GALTON, FRANCIS. *Narrative of an Explorer in Tropical South Africa*. London: John Murray, 1853.

GARDINER, CAPTAIN ALLEN F. *Narrative of a Journey to the Zoolu Country*. London: William Crofts, 1836.

HAKLUYT, RICHARD. *Voyages*. Vols. IV, VI, VII, and XI. Glasgow: Maclehose and Sons, 1904.

HARRIS, SIR WILLIAM CORNWALLIS. *The Wild Sports of Southern Africa*. London: John Murray, 1839.

HUTCHINSON, T. J. *Narrative of the Niger, Tshadda, and Binue Exploration*. London: Longman, Brown, Green and Longmans, 1855.

JOBSON, RICHARD. *The Golden Trade, or a Discovery of the River Gambia*. London: Nicholas Okes, 1623.

LAING, ALEXANDER GORDON. *Travels in the Timannee, Kooranko and Soolima Countries*. London: John Murray, 1825.

LAIRD, MACGREGOR and R. A. K. OLDFIELD. *Narrative of an Expedition in the Interior of Africa by the River Niger in 1832–34*. London: John Murray, 1837.

LANDER, RICHARD and JOHN. *Journal of an Expedition to Explore the Course and Termination of the Niger*. 2 vols. New York: J. and J. Harper, 1833.

LIVINGSTONE, DAVID. *Missionary Travels and Researches in South Africa*. New York: Harper and Brothers, 1859.

MASON, JOHN. *Life with the Zulus of Natal*. London: Longman, Brown, Green and Longmans, 1855.

METHUEN, HENRY E. *Life in the Wilderness, or Wanderings in South Africa.* London: Richard Bentley, 1846.

MOFFAT, ROBERT. *Matabele Journals.* 2 vols. London: Chatto and Windus, 1945 (first published in 1855).

———. *Missionary Labours and Scenes in Southern Africa.* New York: Robert Carter, 1842.

MURRAY, HUGH, ROBERT JAMESON and JAMES WILSON. *Narrative of Discovery and Adventure in Africa.* London: Thomas Nelson, 1849 (first published in 1830).

NORRIS, ROBERT. *Memoirs of the Reign of Bossa Ahadee, King of Dahomey.* London, 1789.

PARK, MUNGO. *Journal of a Mission to the Interior of Africa in the year 1805, to which is prefixed an Account of the Life of Mr. Park by J. Whishaw.* Philadelphia: Edward Earle, 1815.

———. *Travels in the Interior Districts of Africa, 1795, 1796, and 1797.* London: J. M. Dent and Co. n.d. (first published in 1799).

PRINGLE, THOMAS. *African Sketches.* London, 1834.

PURCHAS, SAMUEL. *Purchas His Pilgrimes.* Vol. VI. Glasgow: James Maclehose and Sons, 1905.

RANKIN, F. HARRISON. *The White Man's Grave: A Visit to Sierra Leone in 1834.* 2 vols. London: John Murray, 1836.

SMITH, WILLIAM. *A New Voyage to Guinea.* London, 1744.

SNELGRAVE, WILLIAM. *A New Account of Some Parts of Guinea and the Slave Trade.* London, 1734.

STEEDMAN, ANDREW. *Wanderings and Adventures in the Interior of Southern Africa.* 2 vols. London: Longmans and Co., 1835.

THOMPSON, THOMAS. "An Account of Two Missionary Voyages," in F. Wolfson, *Pageant of Ghana.* London: Oxford University Press, 1958.

Chapter II. The Dawn of Empire

ASHE, ROBERT P. *Two Kings of Uganda.* London: Sampson Low and Co., 1890.

BAKER, SIR SAMUEL W. *Ismailia, a Narrative of the Expedition to Central Africa for the Suppression of the Slave Trade.* 2 vols. London: Macmillan, 1874.

———. *Albert N'Yanza.* 2 vols. London: Macmillan, 1866.

BURTON, SIR RICHARD FRANCIS. *A Mission to Gelele, King of Dahomey.* 2 vols. London: Tinsley Brothers, 1877.

———. *The Lake Regions of Central Africa.* 2 vols. New York: Horizon Press, 1961; reprinted from the original edition of 1861.

————. *First Footsteps in East Africa*. London and New York: Everyman's Edition, 1910 (first published in 1856).

CAMERON, VERNEY LOVETT. *Across Africa (1873–1876)*. New York: Harper and Brothers, 1877.

ELTON, JAMES FREDERICK. *Journals of Travels and Researches among the Lakes and Mountains of Eastern and Central Africa*. Edited and compiled by M. B. COTTERILL. London: John Murray, 1879.

HINDERER, ANNA. *Seventeen Years in the Yoruba Country. Memorials gathered from her journals and letters*. London: Seeley, Jackson and Halliday, 1872.

JOHNSTON, SIR HARRY H. *The Kilimanjaro Expedition*. London: Kegan Paul, Trench and Co., 1886.

————. *The River Congo, from its mouth to Bolobo*. London: Sampson Low, Marston, Searle and Rivington, 1884.

LIVINGSTONE, DAVID. *The Last Journals of David Livingstone in Central Africa from 1865 to his death*. New York: Harper and Brothers, 1875.

————. *Narrative of an Expedition to the Zambesi and its Tributaries; and of the discovery of the Lakes Shirwa and Nyassa, 1858–1864*. New York: Harper and Brothers, 1866.

PETHERICK, JOHN. *Egypt, the Soudan and Central Africa*. Edinburgh and London: W. Blackwood and Sons, 1861.

———— with MRS. PETHERICK. *Travels in Central Africa and Explorations of the Western Nile Tributaries*. 2 vols. London: Tinsley Brothers, 1869.

READE, WINWOOD W. *Savage Africa*. New York: Harper and Brothers, 1864.

SPEKE, JOHN HANNING. *Journey of the Discovery of the Source of the Nile*. New York: J. and J. Harper, 1864.

STANLEY, HENRY M. *Coomassie and Magdala: The story of two British campaigns in Africa*. New York: Harper and Brothers, 1874.

————. *How I Found Livingstone: travels, adventures, and discoveries in Central Africa, including an account of four months' residence with Dr. Livingstone*. 2 vols. New York: Charles Scribner, 1890.

————. *In Darkest Africa, or the Quest, Rescue and Retreat of Emin, Governor of Equatoria*. 2 vols. New York, Charles Scribner, 1890.

————. *Through the Dark Continent, or, The Sources of the Nile Around the Great Lakes of Equatorial Africa*. 2 vols. London, 1899 (first published in 1878).

THOMSON, J. B. *Joseph Thomson, African Explorer*. London: Sampson Low, Marston and Co., 1896.

THOMSON, JOSEPH. *Through Masailand*. London: Sampson Low, Marston, Searle and Rivington, 1885.

———. *To the Central African Lakes and Back*. 2 vols. 2nd. ed. Boston: Houghton Mifflin and Co., 1881.

Chapter III. The Height of Empire

ALLDRIDGE, THOMAS J. *A Transformed Colony, Sierra Leone, As it was and as it is*. . . . London: Seeley and Co., 1910.

ARKELL-HARDWICK, A. *An Ivory Trader in North Kenia*. London: Longmans, Green and Co., 1903.

BALFOUR, ALICE BLANCHE. *Twelve Hundred Miles in a Waggon*. London: Edward Arnold, 1895.

BATEMAN, LATROBE C. S. *The Ascent of the Kasai*. New York: Dodd, Mead and Co., 1889.

BOISRAGON, CAPTAIN ALAN. *The Benin Massacre*. London: Methuen and Co., 1897.

BRYCE, JAMES. *Impressions of South Africa*. New York: The Century Co., 1897.

CHURCHILL, WINSTON S. *My African Journey*. London: Hodder and Stoughton, 1908.

COOPER-CHADWICK, J. *Three Years with Lobengula and Experiences in South Africa*. London: Cassell and Co., 1894.

DECLÉ, LIONEL. *Three Years in Savage Africa*. Introduction by H. M. Stanley, London: Methuen and Co., 1898.

DIXIE, LADY FLORENCE. *In the Land of Misfortune*. London: Richard Bentley and Son, 1882.

DOYLE, ARTHUR CONAN. *The Great Boer War*. New York: McClure, Phillips, 1900.

FREEMAN, RICHARD AUSTIN. *Travels and Life in Ashanti and Jaman*. London: Archibald Constable and Co., 1898.

GLAVE, E. J. *In Savage Africa; or Six Years of Adventure in Congoland*. New York: R. H. Russell and Son, 1892.

GROGAN, EWART S. and ARTHUR H. SHARP. *From the Cape to Cairo*. London: Hurst and Blackett, 1900.

HAGGARD, H. RIDER. *Cetywayo and His White Neighbours*. London: Trubner and Co., 1882.

HALL, MARY. *A Woman's Trek from the Cape to Cairo*. London: Methuen and Co., 1907.

HORE, ANNIE B. *To Lake Tanganyika in a Bath Chair*. London, 1886.

JOHNSTON, SIR HARRY H. *The Story of My Life.* New York: Bobbs, Merrill and Co., 1923.

————. *The Uganda Protectorate.* 2 vols. London: Hutchinson and Co., 1902.

————. *British Central Africa.* New York: Edward Arnold, 1897.

KINGSLEY, MARY. *West African Studies.* London: Macmillan and Co., 1899.

————. *Travels in West Africa.* London: Macmillan and Co., 1898.

KIPLING, RUDYARD. *Something of Myself.* New York: Doubleday, Doran and Co., 1937.

————. *Letters of Travel 1892–1913.* New York: 1927 (first published in 1914).

LARYMORE, CONSTANCE. *A Resident's Wife in Nigeria.* London: George Rutledge and Sons, 1908.

LEONARD, MAJOR ARTHUR GLYN. *How We Made Rhodesia.* London: Kegan Paul, Trench, Trubner and Co., 1896.

LUGARD, FREDERICK D. *The Dual Mandate in British Tropical Africa.* Edinburgh and London: W. Blackwood and Sons, 1929.

————. *The Rise of Our East African Empire.* 2 vols. Edinburgh and London: W. Blackwood and Sons, 1893.

LUGARD, LADY FLORA. *A Tropical Dependency: An Outline of the Ancient History of the Western Soudan, with an account of the modern settlement of Northern Nigeria.* London: J. Nisbet and Co., 1905.

MACDONALD, MAJOR J. R. L. *Soldiering and Surveying in British East Africa, 1891–1894.* London: Edward Arnold, 1897.

MACKAY, A. M. *Mackay of Uganda.* New York: A. C. Armstrong and Son, 1890.

MACKENZIE, JOHN. *Day-Dawn in Dark Places.* London: Cassell and Company, 1883.

PRINGLE, MRS. M. A. *Towards the Mountains of the Moon.* Edinburgh and London: W. Blackwood and Sons, 1883.

ROBINSON, CHARLES H. *Nigeria, Our Latest Protectorate.* New York: Oakside Press, 1900.

————. *Hausaland.* London: Sampson Low, Marston and Co., 1896.

SELOUS, F. COURTENAY. *Travel and Adventure in South East Africa.* London: Rowland Ward and Co., 1893.

SWANN, ALFRED J. *Fighting the Slave Hunters in Central Africa.* London: Seeley and Co., 1910.

TUCKER, BISHOP ALFRED R. *Eighteen Years in Uganda and East Africa.* 2 vols. London: Edward Arnold, 1908.

VANDELEUR, SEYMOUR. *Campaigning on the Upper Nile and Niger.* Introduction by G. T. Goldie. London: Methuen and Co., 1898.

WHITE, ARTHUR SILVA. *The Development of Africa.* London: George Philip and Son, 1890.

WORSFOLD, BASIL W. *A History of South Africa.* London: J. M. Dent and Co., 1900.

THE FICTION TO 1910

BEHN, APHRA. "Oroonoko," in *The Shorter Novels of Aphra Behn.* Vol. II. London: Everyman's Edition, 1929 (first published around 1677).

BUCHAN, JOHN. *Prester John.* Boston and New York: Houghton Mifflin Co., 1928 (first published in 1910).

CHALMERS, JOHN. *Fighting the Matabele.* London: 1898.

CONRAD, JOSEPH. *Heart of Darkness.* New York: Signet, 1961 (first published in 1899).

————. "An Outpost of Progress," in *Tales Of Unrest.* New York: Doubleday, Page and Co., 1925 (first published in 1898).

DODD, REVEREND WILLIAM. "The Epistle of Zara at the Court of Anamaboe, to the African Prince now in England," in *Dodsley's Collections.* Vol. IV. London, 1783.

FITZPATRICK, SIR PERCY. *Jock of the Bushveld.* London: Longmans, Green and Co., n.d. (first published in 1907).

GAUNT, MARY. *The Uncounted Cost.* London, 1904.

GLANVILLE, ERNEST. *The Fossicker, A Romance of Mashonaland.* London: Chatto and Windus, 1891.

HAGGARD, H. RIDER. *Nada The Lily.* London, 1892.

————. *Allan Quatermain.* New York: Dover, 1951 (first published in 1888).

————. *She.* New York: Dover, 1951 (first published in 1887).

————. *Jess.* New York: Longmans, Green and Co., 1918 (first published in 1887).

————. *King Solomon's Mines.* New York: Dover, 1951 (first published in 1886).

HENTY, G. A. *Young Colonists.* New York: F. M. Lupton Co., n.d. (first published in 1888).

KIPLING, RUDYARD. *Traffics and Discoveries.* New York: Doubleday and Co., 1927 (first published in 1904).

MARRYAT, CAPTAIN FREDERICK. *The Privateersman.* Boston: Roberts Brothers, 1866.

——. *The Mission, or Scenes in Africa.* London: J. M. Dent and Co., 1845.

MAUGHAM, SOMERSET. *The Explorer.* New York: George H. Doran Company, 1907.

MITFORD, SIR BERTRAM. *The King's Assegai.* London, 1895.

——. *John Ames, Native Commissioner, or a Romance of the Matabele Uprising.* London: F. V. White and Company, 1900.

READE, CHARLES. *A Simpleton.* Boston and New York: Colonia Press, n.d. (first published in 1873).

READE, WINWOOD W. *African Sketchbooks.* 2 vols. London: Smith, Elder and Co., 1873.

SCHREINER, OLIVE. *Story of an African Farm.* New York: A. L. Burt, n.d. (first published in 1883).

SCULLY, WILLIAM CHARLES. *Kaffir Stories.* London: 1895.

SKERTCHLY, J. A. *Melinda the Caboceer, or Sport in Ashanti.* New York: D. Appleton and Co., 1876.

STANLEY, HENRY M. *My Kalulu.* New York: Scribner, Armstrong and Co., 1874.

WALLACE, EDGAR. *Sanders of the River.* Garden City: Doubleday, Doran and Co., 1930 (first published in 1909).

THE BRITISH EMPIRE AND VICTORIANISM

This bibliography makes no attempt to list all the books about the Victorian era, only those to which there is direct reference, or those of sufficient significance to warrant inclusion in such a brief listing. The interested reader can easily find himself inundated with Victoriana merely for the looking. Our concern was directed primarily to those works about the literature of the Victorian period and about the British Empire.

BAKER, JOSEPH E. *The Reinterpretation of Victorian Literature.* Princeton: Princeton University Press, 1950.

BRIGGS, ASA. *Victorian People.* Chicago: University of Chicago Press, 1955.

British Broadcasting Corporation. *Ideas and Beliefs of the Victorians.* London: 1949.

BUCKLEY, JEROME H. *The Victorian Temper: A Study in Literary Culture.* Cambridge: Harvard University Press, 1951.

Cambridge History of English Literature. Vols. XII and XIV. Cambridge University Press, 1953.

COLE, G. D. H. and RAYMOND POSTGATE. *The British Common People, 1746–1938.* New York: Alfred A. Knopf, 1939.

CRUSE, AMY. *The Victorians and Their Books.* London: Allen and Unwin, 1935.

DALZIEL, MARGARET. *Popular Fiction 100 Years Ago.* London: Cohen and West, 1957.

DILKE, SIR CHARLES. *The British Empire.* London: Chatto and Windus, 1899.

————. *Great Britain: A Record of Travel in English Speaking Countries in 1866 and 1867.* London: Macmillan and Co., 1872.

HALÉVY, ELIE. *A History of the English People in the Nineteenth Century,* translated from French by E. I. Watkin and D. A. Baker. 6 vols. New York: Barnes and Noble, 1961.

HALL, WINIFRED. *The Overseas Empire in Fiction.* London: Oxford University Press, 1942.

HOBSON, J. A. *Imperialism, A Study.* London: Archibald Constable and Co., 1905.

HOUGHTON, W. E. *The Victorian Frame of Mind, 1830–1870.* New Haven: Yale University Press, 1957.

HOWE, SUSAN. *Novels of Empire.* New York: Columbia University Press, 1949.

LUCAS, SIR CHARLES. *The British Empire.* London: Macmillan, 1924.

NOTESTEIN, WALLACE. *The Scot in History.* New Haven: Yale University Press, 1949.

PETRIE, SIR CHARLES. *The Victorians.* London: Eyre and Spottiswoode, 1960.

ROBINSON, RONALD and J. GALLAGHER, with ALICE DENNY. *Africa and the Victorians: The Climax of Imperialism in the Dark Continent.* New York: St. Martin's Press, 1961.

SAUNDERS, LAURANCE JAMES. *Scottish Democracy, 1815–1840, The Social and Intellectual Background.* London and Edinburgh: Oliver and Boyd, 1950.

SEELEY, J. R. *The Expansion of England.* London: Macmillan, 1931 (first published in 1883).

THORNTON, A. P. *The Imperial Idea and Its Enemies.* London: Macmillan, 1959.

TINDALL, WILLIAM Y. *Forces in Modern British Literature, 1885–1946.* New York: Alfred A. Knopf, 1947.

WINGFIELD-STRATTON, ESME. *The Victorian Aftermath.* New York: William Morrow and Co., 1934.

————. *The Victorian Sunset.* New York: William Morrow and Co., 1932.

————. *Those Ernest Victorians.* New York: William Morrow and Co., 1930.

YOUNG, G. M. *Victorian England: Portrait of an Age*. London: Oxford University Press, 1936.

———— (ed.). *Early Victorian England*. 2 vols. London: Oxford University Press, 1934.

ZIMMERN, ALFRED. *The Third British Empire*. London: Oxford University Press, 1934.

THE TRADITION IN THE TWENTIETH CENTURY

The listing of books that follows is a selective, working bibliography. The British have written so much on Africa since 1910, and especially since 1930, that we could not include everything we had read, let alone particular books that anyone else had read. Nor were we concerned to list all of any author's output. Our wish was rather to be sufficiently inclusive and wide-ranging to provide an adequate sample.

The bibliographic organization differs from that of the first part of the book; it was not feasible to follow the chapter headings. Though some of the writers adhere strongly to one or the other of the predominant images, too many of them use conventions that are appropriate to several of the images. It is possible to isolate some of the books that deal primarily with the hunting ethos, such as D. R. Sherman's *Into the Noonday Sun*, or Colin Willock's *The Animal Catchers*, but more frequently even the mystique of the hunt is only part of a more eclectic view of Africa in which other themes and images are incorporated. We have, therefore, been content merely to separate out the fiction from the nonfiction.

We have included also a separate list of a selected bibliography of South African novels of social protest. Though not dealt with in the text, they are the most important and probably the best-known novels about Africa in the United States. They are pertinent here in that they carry on the traditional humanitarian line of Olive Schreiner. Some of these novelists move into the area of African imagery in certain of their books or in parts of others. Harry Bloom's *Whittaker's Wife* clearly belongs in the realm of British imagery about Africa, while his *Episode in the Transvaal* is a classic novel of social protest. William Plomer's *Turbott Wolfe* has been called by Laurens Van der Post (Introduction to Turbott Wolfe) one of the pivotal works of South African fiction, combining the traditions of Haggard and Schreiner. It does, indeed, properly belong to the data of the African image as well as to the fiction of social protest.

The work of Pauline Smith has been listed along with the South African material, but hers are novels and tales of social realism rather than social protest, and primarily concern the Afrikaners rather than the British or Africans. Her view of the barren, open veldt and the stolid Boers is in the Schreiner tradition, though she evokes them as few other novelists have done.

Nonfiction

BAKER, RICHARD ST. BARBE. *African Drums*. Revised edition. Oxford: George Ronald, Wheatley Co., 1951.

BIGLAND, EILEEN. *The Lake of the Royall Crocodiles*. New York: Macmillan, 1939.

BINKS, H. K. *African Rainbow*. London: Sidgwick and Jackson, 1959.

BIRKBY, CAROL. *Limpopo Journey*. London: Frederick Miller, 1939.

BLAKE, W. T. *Rhodesia and Nyasaland Journey*. London: Alvin Redman, Ltd., 1960.

BUCHAN, JOHN. *Pilgrim's Way*. Boston: Houghton Mifflin Co., 1940.

CAMPBELL, ROY. *Light on a Dark Horse*. Chicago: Henry Regnery, 1952.

CARY, JOYCE. *The Case for African Freedom*. London: Secker and Warburg, 1944.

CLOETE, STUART. *The African Giant*. Boston: Houghton Mifflin Company, 1955.

COLLINS, DOUGLAS. *A Tear for Somalia*. London: Jarrolds, 1960.

COLLIS, ROBERT. *African Encounter*. New York: Charles Scribner's Sons, 1961.

COLLODON, AUGUSTUS C. *Congo Jake*. New York: Claude Kendall, 1933.

———. *Congo Jake Returns*. London: John Long, 1934.

CRANWORTH, LORD. *Kenya Chronicles*. London: Macmillan, 1939.

DICKSON, MORA. *New Nigerians*. London: Dennis Dobson, 1960.

DINESEN, ISAK. *Out of Africa*. New York: Random House, 1938.

———. *Shadows on the Grass*. New York: Random House, 1961.

DUNDAS, SIR CHARLES. *African Crossroads*. London: Macmillan, 1955.

DURRELL, GERALD M. *The Overloaded Ark*. New York: The Viking Press, 1953.

GIBBS, PETER. *A Flag for the Matabele*. New York: Vanguard, 1956.

GORER, GEOFFREY. *Africa Dances*. London: John Lehmann, 1949.

GOULDSBURY, CULLEN. *An African Year*. London: Edward Arnold, 1912.

GREEN, LAWRENCE G. *Lands of the Last Frontier: The Story of South West Africa and Its People of All Races*. London: Stanley Paul and Co., 1953.

GREENE, GRAHAM. *In Search of a Character: Two African Journals*. New York: Viking Press, 1961.

————. *Journey Without Maps.* New York: Compass, 1961 (first published in 1936).

HAGGARD, H. RIDER. *The Days of My Life.* 2 vols. London: Longmans, Green and Co., 1926.

HASTINGS, A. C. G. *Nigerian Days.* London: John Lane, 1925.

HENDERSON, IAN. *Manhunt in Kenya.* Garden City: Doubleday, 1958.

HENNINGS, R. D. *African Morning.* London: Chatto and Windus, 1951.

HIVES, FRANK and LUMLEY GASCOINE. *Ju-Ju and Justice in Nigeria.* New York: Ballantine Books, 1961.

HOARE, RAWDON. *Rhodesian Mosaic.* London: John Murray, 1934.

HORN, ALOYSIUS and E. LEWIS. *Trader Horn.* New York: Grosset and Dunlap, 1927.

HUNTER, J. A. *Hunter.* New York: Harper and Bros., 1952.

———— and DANIEL P. MANNIX. *Tales of the African Frontier.* New York: Harper and Bros., 1954.

HUXLEY, ELSPETH. *On the Edge of the Rift.* New York: William Morrow and Co., 1962.

————. *A New Earth.* New York: William Morrow and Co., 1960.

————. *The Flame Trees of Thika.* New York: William Morrow and Co., 1959.

————. *Four Guineas.* London: Chatto and Windus, 1954.

————. *The Sorcerer's Apprentice.* London: Chatto and Windus, 1949.

JACKSON, SIR FREDERICK. *Early Days in East Africa.* London: Edward Arnold and Co., 1930.

JACKSON, H. C. *Sudan Days and Ways.* London: Macmillan, 1954.

JARRETT-KERR, MARTIN. *African Pulse.* London: Faith Press, 1960.

MARKHAM, BERYL. *West with the Night.* Boston: Houghton Mifflin and Co., 1942.

MARSH, JOHN and LYMAN ANSON. *Skeleton Coast.* New York: Dodd, Mead and Co., 1958.

MATURIN, EDITH. *Adventures Beyond the Zambesi.* London: Eveleigh Nash, 1913.

MAUGHAM, ROBIN. *The Slaves of Timbuktu.* New York: Harper and Brothers, 1961.

MICHAEL, MARJORIE. *I Married a Hunter.* New York: G. P. Putnam's Sons, 1957.

MILLS, LADY DOROTHY. *Road to Timbuktu.* London: Duckworth and Co., 1924.

————. *The Golden Land.* London: Duckworth and Co., 1926.

MOCKFORD, JULIAN. *Golden Land.* London: Adam and Charles Black, 1949.

MORTON, H. V. *In Search of South Africa*. London: Methuen and Co., 1948.

MOTLEY, MARY. *Devils in Waiting*. London: Longmans, Green and Co., 1959.

NEAL, JAMES H. *Jungle Magic*. New York: David McKay, 1966.

NEVINSON, HENRY W. *More Changes More Chances*. New York: Harcourt, Brace and Co., 1925.

PACKER, JOY. *Apes and Ivory*. London: Eyre and Spottiswoode, 1953.

PATTERSON, JOHN HENRY. *The Man-Eaters of Tsavo and Other African Adventures*. New York: Macmillan, 1927.

PLOMER, WILLIAM. *Double Lives*. New York: Noonday Press, 1956.

POWYS, LLEWELLYN. *Ebony and Ivory*. New York: Harcourt, Brace and Co., 1923.

PRETORIUS, MAJOR P. J. *Jungle Man*. New York: E. P. Dutton and Co., 1948.

RANIER, PETER. *My Vanished Africa*. New Haven: Yale University Press, 1940.

RAYNE, MAJOR H. *Sun, Sand and Somals*. London: H. F. and G. Witherby, 1921.

READ, GRANTLY DICK. *No Time for Fear*. New York: Harper and Bros., 1955.

REDMAYNE, SIR RICHARD. *Men, Mines and Memories*. London: Eyre and Spottiswoode, 1942.

REEVE, ALAN. *Africa, I Presume*. New York: Macmillan, 1948.

RYAN, MARGARET G. *African Hayride*. New York: Rand McNally, 1956.

SCOBIE, ALASTAIR. *Women of Africa*. London: Cassell and Co., 1960.

SCULLY, WILLIAM CHARLES. *Further Reminiscences of a South African Pioneer*. London: Fischer Unwin, 1913.

————. *Reminiscences of a South African Pioneer*. London: Fischer Unwin, 1911.

SEYMOUR, JOHN. *One Man's Africa*. New York: John Day, 1956.

SIMPSON, ALYSE. *The Red Dust of Kenya*. New York: Thomas Y. Crowell Co., 1952.

SMITH, ANTHONY. *High Street Africa*. London: Allen and Unwin, 1961.

STATHAM, COL. J. C. B. *With My Wife Across Africa By Canoe and Caravan*. London: Simpkin, Marshall, Hamilton, Kent and Co., 1924.

SWEENEY, R. C. H. *The Scurrying Bush*. New York: Random House, 1965.

TAYLOR, JOHN. *Maneaters and Marauders*. New York: A. S. Barnes and Co., 1960.

TONG, RAYMOND. *Figures in Ebony.* London: Cassell and Co., 1958.
VAN DER POST, LAURENS. *The Heart of the Hunter.* New York: William Morrow and Co., 1961.
————. "Portrait of a Continent," *Holiday,* April 1959.
————. *The Dark Eye in Africa.* New York: William Morrow and Co., 1955.
————. *Venture to the Interior.* New York: William Morrow and Co., 1951.
WYKES, ALAN. *Snake-Man.* New York: Simon and Schuster, 1961.
WYNDHAM, RICHARD. *The Gentle Savage.* New York: William Morrow and Co., 1936.

Fiction

ALLAN, RALPH. *Ask the Name of the Lion.* New York: Doubleday and Co., 1962.
AMBLER, ERIC. *Dirty Story.* New York: Atheneum, 1967.
BAKER, RICHARD ST. BARBE. *Kabongo.* Oxford: George Ronald Co., 1955.
BEAVON, ERIC A. *Sindiga the Savage.* London: Harpers, 1930.
BINDLOSS, HAROLD. *The League of the Leopard.* London, 1923.
Blackwood Magazine, collections from. "Tales from the Outposts." Vol. V. *Jobs of Work.* Edinburgh and London: William Blackwood and Sons, 1932.
BLOOM, HARRY. *Whittaker's Wife.* New York: Simon and Schuster, 1962.
BROOK, IAN. *The Black List.* New York: G. P. Putnam's Sons, 1962.
————. *Jimmy Riddle.* New York: G. P. Putnam's Sons, 1961.
BUCHAN, JOHN. *The Island of Sheep.* London, 1936.
————. *The Runagates Club.* London, 1928.
BURGESS, ANTHONY. *Devil of a State.* New York: W. W. Norton and Co., 1961.
CAMERON, RODERICK. *Equator Farm.* New York: Roy, 1956.
CANAWAY, W. H. *Find the Boy.* New York: Viking Press, 1961.
CANNING, VICTOR. *The Burning Eye.* New York: William Sloane Associates, 1960.
CARY, JOYCE. *Aissa Saved.* Carfax Edition. London, 1952.
————. *An American Visitor.* Carfax Edition, 1952.
————. *Mr. Johnson.* New York: Berkley Medallion Books, 1961.
————. *Spring Song.* New York: Harper and Bros., 1960.
————. *The African Witch.* Carfax Edition. London, 1951.
————. *Castle Corner.* London: Michael Joseph, 1938.

CATTO, MAX. *Mr. Moses.* New York: William Morrow and Co., 1961.
————. *Gold in the Sky.* New York: William Morrow and Co., 1958.
CAUTE, DAVID. *Decline of the West.* New York: Macmillan, 1966.
————. *At Fever Pitch.* New York: Pantheon, 1961.
CLOETE, STUART. *Gazella.* New York: Pocket Books, 1959.
————. *Congo Song.* New York: Monarch, 1958.
DRUMMOND, JUNE. *Welcome, Proud Lady.* New York: Holt, Rinehart and Winston, 1968.
FORESTER, C. S. *The Sky and the Forest.* Boston: Little, Brown and Co., 1948.
————. *The African Queen.* New York: Bantam Books, 1960.
GLANVILLE, ERNEST. *The Hunter, A Story of Bushmen.* New York: Harcourt, Brace and Co., 1926.
GREENE, GRAHAM. *The Heart of the Matter.* New York: The Viking Press, 1948.
————. *A Burnt-Out Case.* New York: The Viking Press, 1961.
GRIFFIN, GWYN. *Something of an Achievement.* New York: Henry Holt and Co., 1960.
————. *By the North Gate.* New York: Henry Holt and Co., 1959.
HANLEY, GERALD. *Gilligan's Last Elephant.* Cleveland: World, 1962.
————. *Drinkers of Darkness.* New York: Macmillan, 1955.
————. *The Year of the Lion.* New York: Macmillan, 1954.
HARDY, RONALD. *The Savages.* New York: G. P. Putnam's Sons, 1967.
————. *The Men from the Bush.* Garden City: Doubleday and Co., 1959.
HENRIQUES, ROBERT D. Q. *Death by Moonlight.* New York: William Morrow and Co., 1938.
HOLTBY, WINIFRED. *Mandoa, Mandoa!* New York: Macmillan, 1933.
HORNE, GEOFFREY. *The Man Who Was Chief.* London: Chapman and Hall, 1960.
HUXLEY, ELSPETH. *The Red Rock Wilderness.* New York: William Morrow and Co., 1957.
————. *The Walled City.* Philadelphia and New York: J. B. Lippincott Co., 1949.
JENKINS, GEOFFREY. *A Twist of Sand.* New York: Viking Press, 1960.
LAIT, ROBERT. *Massacre at Tangini.* New York: Random House, 1963.
————. *Honey for Tomorrow.* New York: Random House, 1961.
LANE, MARGARET. *A Calabash of Diamonds.* New York: Duell, Sloan and Pearce, 1961.
LLEWELLYN, RICHARD. *A Man in a Mirror.* New York: Doubleday and Co., 1961.
LODWICK, JOHN. *Equator.* London: Heinemann, 1957.

MATHEW, DAVID. *The Mango on the Mango Tree*. New York: Alfred A. Knopf, 1951.

MILLIN, SARAH GERTRUDE. *The Herr Witchdoctor*. London: William Heinemann, 1941.

————. *God's Stepchildren*. New York: Boni and Liveright, 1924.

————. *Adam's Rest*. London, 1922.

MILNE, SHIRLEY. *Beware the Lurking Scorpion*. London: House and Maxwell, 1966.

MONSARRAT, NICHOLAS. *The Tribe that Lost Its Head*. New York: William Sloane Associates, 1956.

MUNDY, TALBOT. *The Ivory Trail*. Indianapolis: Bobbs, Merrill Co., 1919.

NEAME, ALAN. *The Adventures of Maud Noakes*. New York: New Directions, 1960.

PACKER, JOY. *The Glass Barrier*. Philadelphia: J. B. Lippincott, 1961.

PLOMER, WILLIAM. *Turbott Wolfe*. New York: William Morrow, 1965 (first published in 1926).

RAND, JAMES. *Run for the Trees*. New York: Putnam, 1967.

REID, VICTOR STAFFORD. *The Leopard*. New York: Viking Press, 1958.

ROOKE, DAPHNE. *A Lover for Estelle*. Boston: Houghton Mifflin Co., 1961.

————. *Wizard's Country*. Cambridge, Mass.: Riverside Press, 1957.

SCHOLEFIELD, ALAN. *Great Elephant*. New York: William Morrow and Co., 1968.

————. *A View of Vultures*. London: Heinemann, 1966.

SCHOLEY, JEAN. *The Dead Past*. New York: Macmillan, 1962.

SHAW, ROBERT. *The Sun Doctor*. New York: Harcourt, Brace and World, 1961.

SHERMAN, D. R. *Into the Noonday Sun*. Boston: Little, Brown and Co., 1966.

SMITH, WILBUR. *The Train from Katanga*. New York: Viking, 1965.

STACEY, TOM. *The Brothers M*. New York: Pantheon Books, 1961.

STEEN, MARGUERITE. *Twilight on the Floods*. Garden City: Doubleday and Co., 1949.

————. *The Sun Is My Undoing*. New York: Viking Press, 1941.

TREVOR, ELLESTON. *The Freebooters*. Garden City: Doubleday and Co., 1967.

VAN DER POST, LAURENS. *The Hunter and the Whale*. New York: William Morrow and Co., 1967.

————. *Flamingo Feather*. New York: William Morrow and Co., 1955.

VIERTEL, PETER. *White Hunter, Black Heart*. London: W. H. Allen, 1954.

WALLACE, EDGAR. *Mr. Commissioner Sanders.* New York: Doubleday, Doran and Co., 1930.

WAUGH, EVELYN. *Black Mischief.* New York: Dell Publishing Co., 1960.

WILLOCK, COLIN. *The Animal Catchers.* New York: Doubleday and Co., 1964.

WILSON, JOHN ROWAN. *The Double Blind.* New York: Doubleday and Co., 1960.

YOUNG, FRANCIS BRETT. *The City of Gold.* London: William Heinemann, 1939.

————. *They Seek a Country.* Baltimore: Waverly Press, 1937.

South African Fiction of Social Protest

ABRAHAMS, PETER. *A Wreath for Udomo.* New York: Alfred A. Knopf, 1956.

————. *Mine Boy.* New York: Alfred A. Knopf, 1955.

————. *Tell Freedom.* New York: Alfred A. Knopf, 1954.

BLOOM, HARRY. *Episode in the Transvaal.* London: Collins, 1956.

COPE, JACK. *The Tame Ox.* London: William Heinemann, 1960.

————. *The Golden Oriole.* London: William Heinemann, 1958.

GORDIMER, NADINE. *Friday's Footprints.* New York: Simon and Schuster, 1960.

————. *A World of Strangers.* New York: Simon and Schuster, 1958.

————. *Six Feet of the Country.* New York: Simon and Schuster, 1956.

————. *The Lying Days.* New York: Simon and Schuster, 1953.

————. *Soft Voice of the Serpent.* New York: Simon and Schuster, 1952.

JACOBSON, DAN. *The Zulu and the Zeide.* Boston: Little, Brown and Co., 1959.

————. *The Evidence of Love.* Boston: Little, Brown and Co., 1959.

————. *The Price of Diamonds.* London: Weidenfeld and Nicolson, 1957.

————. *A Dance in the Sun.* London: Weidenfeld and Nicolson, 1956.

KRIGE, UYS. *The Dream and the Desert.* London: Collins, 1953.

LESSING, DORIS. *Martha Quest and a Proper Marriage* (volumes 1 and 2 of *Children of Violence*). New York, 1965.

————. *A Ripple from the Storm and Landlocked* (volumes 3 and 4 of *Children of Violence*). New York, 1966.

————. *African Stories.* London: Michael Joseph, 1964.

————. *Five Short Novels.* London: Michael Joseph, 1953.

————.*This Was the Old Chief's Country*. London: Michael Joseph, 1952.

————. *The Grass Is Singing*. London: Michael Joseph, 1950.

PATON, ALAN. *Tales from a Troubled Land*. New York: Charles Scribner's Sons, 1964.

————. *Too Late the Phalarope*. New York: Charles Scribner's Sons, 1953.

————. *Cry, the Beloved Country*. New York: Charles Scribner's Sons, 1948.

SMITH, PAULINE. *The Beadle*. New York: Vanguard, 1954 (first published in 1927).

————. *The Little Karoo*. New York: Vanguard, 1952 (first published in 1926).

The British on Themselves

BELLOC, HILAIRE. *An Essay on the Nature of Contemporary England*. New York: Sheed and Ward, 1937.

BRADBURY, MALCOLM. "The Taste for Anarchy," *Saturday Review*, June 30, 1962.

BROGAN, DENIS W. *The English People—Impressions and Observations*. New York: Alfred A. Knopf, 1943.

CARR, PHILIP. *The English Are Like That*. New York: Charles Scribner's Sons, 1941.

CHAUDHURI, MRAD C. *A Passage to England*. New York: St. Martin's Press, 1959.

CHESSER, EUSTACE. *The Sexual, Marital and Family Relationships of the English Woman*. New York: Roy Publishers, 1957.

COLE, G. D. H. "The Idea of Progress," *British Journal of Sociology*, IV (1953), 266–85.

————. *The Post-War Condition of Britain*. London: Routledge and Kegan Paul, 1956.

DENNIS, NORMAN, FERNANDO HENRIQUES and CLIFFORD SLAUGHTER. *Coal Is Our Life*. London: Eyre and Spottiswoode, 1956.

FARBER, MAURICE L. "English and Americans: A Study of National Character," *Journal of Psychology*, XXXII (1951).

————. "English and Americans: Values in the Socialization Process," *Journal of Psychology*, XXXVI (1953).

FROST, DAVID and ANTONY JAY. *The English*. New York: Stein and Day, 1968.

GLASS, DAVID VICTOR (ed.). *Social Mobility in Britain*. Glencoe: The Free Press, 1954.

GORER, GEOFFREY. *Exploring English Character*. New York: Criterion Books, 1955.

GREEN, MARTIN. *A Mirror for Anglo-Saxons: A Discovery of America, a rediscovery of England*. New York: Harper and Brothers, 1960.

GUTTSMAN, W. L. "Aristocracy and the Middle Class in the British Political Elite 1886–1916," *British Journal of Sociology*, V (1954).

KERR, MADELINE. *The People of Ship Street*. London: Routledge and Kegan Paul, 1958.

LEWIS, ROY and ANGUS MAUDE. *Professional People in England*. Cambridge: Harvard University Press, 1953.

LOGAN, R. F. L. and E. M. GOLDBERG. "Rising Eighteen in a London Suburb," *British Journal of Sociology*, IV (1953), 323–45.

MACK, JOHN. "Review of Gorer—*Exploring English Character*," *British Journal of Sociology*, VI (1955).

DE MADARIAGA, SALVADOR. *Englishmen, Frenchmen and Spaniards*. London: Oxford University Press, 1929.

MARSH, DAVID C. *The Changing Social Structure of England and Wales, 1871–1951*. London: Routledge and Kegan Paul, 1958.

MEAD, MARGARET. *The Application of Anthropological Techniques to Cross-Cultural Communication. Transactions of the New York Academy of Science*. Series 2, no. 9 (1947).

MILLER, S. M. "Comparative Social Mobility," *Current Sociology*, IX, no. 1 (1960).

MITFORD, NANCY. *Noblesse Oblige*. New York: Harper and Bros., 1956.

MOGEY, JOHN. *Family and Neighbourhood*. London: Oxford University Press, 1956.

NICOLSON, HAROLD. *Good Behaviour*. Garden City: Doubleday and Co., 1956.

ORWELL, GEORGE. *The Road to Wigan Pier*. New York: Berkeley Publishing Co., 1961.

———. *A Collection of Essays*. Garden City: Doubleday Anchor Books, 1954.

PEAR, T. H. *English Social Differences*. London: George Allen and Unwin, 1955.

ROWNTREE, B. SEEBOHM and G. R. LAVERS. *English Life and Leisure*. London: Longmans, Green and Co., 1951.

SCOTT, J. D. *Life In Britain*. New York: William Morrow and Co., 1955.

SLATER, ELIOT and MOYA WOODSIDE. *Patterns of Marriage*. London: Cassell and Co., 1951.

SMELLIE, K. B. *The British Way of Life*. London: William Heinemann, 1955.

SPINLEY, B. M. *The Deprived and the Privileged: Personality Development in English Society.* London: Routledge and Kegan Paul, 1953.

STERLING, PAUL. "Review: *Exploring English Character,* Geoffrey Gorer," *American Anthropologist,* LVIII, no. 6 (1956).

STRACHEY, JOHN. *The End of Empire.* New York: Random House, 1960.

TITMUSS, RICHARD M. *Essays on "The Welfare State."* London: George Allen and Unwin, 1958.

WELLARD, JAMES HOWARD. *Understanding the English.* New York: McGraw-Hill, 1937.

WILLMOTT, PETER and MICHAEL YOUNG. *Family and Class in a London Suburb.* Routledge and Kegan Paul, 1960.

WOLFENSTEIN, MARTHA and NATHAN A. LEITES. *Movies.* Glencoe: The Free Press, 1950.

index